D0812609

# Birds of Colonial Williamsburg

Christmas,
1989

A HISTORICAL PORTFOLIO

# Birds of Colonial Williamsburg

By ALAN FEDUCCIA

Illustrations of the Birds by H. DOUGLAS PRATT

THE COLONIAL WILLIAMSBURG FOUNDATION

Williamsburg, Virginia

Text © 1989 by The Colonial Williamsburg Foundation
Artwork © 1989 by H. Douglas Pratt

All rights reserved, including the right to reproduce this book or
portions thereof in any form.

Library of Congress Cataloging in Publication Data

Feduccia, J. Alan.
  Birds of colonial Williamsburg: a historical portfolio/by Alan
Feduccia: illustrations of the birds by H. Douglas Pratt.
  p. 166 cm.
    Bibliography: p.
    Includes index.
    ISBN 0-87935-113-6
    1. Birds — Virginia — Williamsburg — History. I. Pratt, H. Douglas
(Harold Douglas), 1944-          . II. Title.
    QL684.V8F43 1989
    598.29755'4252-09033 — dc20                          89-7220

The publication of this book was made possible in part by a gift
from the George L. and Genevieve D. Moore Foundation.

This book was designed by Richard Stinely.

ISBN 0-87935-113-6

Printed and bound in Hong Kong

*Illustrated on the cover, frontispiece, and title page,
respectively, are the Northern Cardinal, Brown Thrasher, and
Carolina Wren.*

# CONTENTS

# INTRODUCTION

JOHN LAWSON and MARK CATESBY were the two most important naturalists to document the ornithology of colonial America in a comprehensive way. The story is more complicated, however, since a number of other naturalists, most of them now obscure, preceded Lawson and Catesby. Much of the natural history of the New World in the colonial period was written by little-known explorers who had a keen interest in the flora and fauna — and perhaps especially the birds — of the Western Hemisphere.

One of the earliest adventurers was John White, the first to draw a series of America's birds. In 1585 White began to paint the illustrations of Indian life in America that became widely known through Theodore de Bry's engravings, which were published in 1588. White also executed thirty-five watercolor drawings of birds, among them the brown pelican, sandhill crane, bald eagle, pileated woodpecker, blue jay, and northern or Baltimore oriole. His bird drawings did not come to light until 1709 when they were discovered in the possession of a descendant.

White made four voyages to the New World. On the second, in 1587, he came as governor of Sir Walter Raleigh's Roanoke colony, bringing one hundred fifty settlers with him, including his daughter and son-in-law, the parents of Virginia Dare, the first English child born in British America. White returned to England and because of political problems did not return to America until 1590, only to learn that the colonists had disappeared. All he found was the word "Croatoan," the name of a friendly Indian tribe, carved into a tree.

Other naturalists wrote bits and pieces about the flora and fauna of colonial America. Thomas Hariot accompanied John White on his second expedition. Hariot's narrative, *A briefe and true report of the new found land of Virginia*, is illustrative of the style of natural history writing of the period: "There are also Parats, Faulcons, and Marlin haukes, which although with us they bee not used for meate, yet for other causes I thought good to mention."

In 1637 Thomas Morton, an Anglican trader who founded a colony, Merry Mount, near Plymouth, Massachusetts, published a book entitled *New English Canaan*. In a ten-page chapter devoted to "Of birds and feathered

The Blue Jay from Mark Catesby, *The Natural History of Carolina, Florida and the Bahama Islands . . . ,* 2 vols. (London, 1731, 1743).

fowles," Morton told of seeing "millions of turtledoves" and "pied ducks" in great abundance.

Perhaps the next major account of birds, aside from the writings of Francisco Hernandes (1514-1578), who dealt primarily with the Mexican biota, was that of John Josselyn (fl. 1630-1675). In his two books, *New England Rarities Discovered* (1672) and *An Account of Two Voyages to New England* (1674), Josselyn was the first to attempt to compile rather extensive lists of birds, beasts, plants, fish, mollusks, and insects of the newly discovered America. For example, he wrote that "of Turkie Cocks, several credible persons affirmed that they weighed forty, yea sixty pound." Josselyn described the *"Vulture"* as "cowardly" because it was seen "preying upon Fish cast upon the shore" and mentioned the *"Gripe"* (the bald eagle). He said that the eagle's quill feathers made excellent text pens and that its tail was "highly esteemed by the *Indians* for their Arrows as they will not sing in flying."

With the advent of John Lawson a more distinctly American period of natural history, including birds, developed. Little is known of Lawson's life, especially his early years. He may have come from London, probably from an aristocratic family of some means. Lawson's own accounts indicate that he was in Rome in 1700 and was told by a gentleman who had been to America that "*Carolina* was the best country I could go to." Thus Lawson departed for the New World, landed at New York, and made his way to Charles Town, South Carolina, where the Lords Proprietors appointed him to explore and survey the interior of the territory known as "Carolina." Lawson's "long voyage" encompassed five hundred fifty miles, lasted fifty-nine days, and ended at a point near present-day Washington, North Carolina. During his lengthy "voyage" Lawson kept an extensive journal with notes on all of the flora and fauna that he encountered.

Lawson quickly rose to prominence in colonial America, being named surveyor-general of North Carolina by the Lords Proprietors. He also became a cofounder of Bath, the oldest town in North Carolina. Lawson returned to London in 1709 to supervise the publication of his book, *A New Voyage to Carolina*. In that year he was appointed, along with Edward Moseley, to be a commissioner on the part of Carolina to survey the territory in dispute with Virginia. When Lawson returned to America in 1710, he thus went to Williamsburg where he encountered the renowned Virginia botanist John Clayton. Unfortunately, only a few months later John Lawson was killed by Tuscarora Indians in the area of New Bern, North Carolina.

Lawson's contribution to the natural history of the New World was enormous. The *New Voyage to Carolina* was the first comprehensive treatise on the natural history of America, and Lawson's list of birds, along with descriptions and observations of many of them, provided the earliest significant ornithology of the region. Lawson's history was devoid of bird illustrations, however, and it remained for Mark Catesby to provide the first major illustrated natural history of America.

Mark Catesby (1682-1749) was born and educated near Essex, England, and was a devoted natural historian since his early days. He came from a prosperous English family. His father, John Catesby, was the magistrate of Sudbury in Suffolk and owned property in London as well as farms and other holdings in Suffolk. Mark Catesby's mother, Elizabeth Jekyll of Castle Hedingham, also belonged to a gentry family, and it was at Castle Hedingham, only sixteen miles from Sudbury, that young Catesby came into contact with many distinguished figures in British natural history circles. For example, the famous Braintree apothecary, Samuel Dale, visited the gardens of Catesby's uncle, Nicholas Jekyll, in 1711, just one year before Catesby set sail for Virginia.

Catesby's sister Elizabeth, who was two years older, played a critical role in his career. Elizabeth married Dr. William Cocke without her father's consent and subsequently went with him to Williamsburg. William Cocke became a success as both a statesman and a physician, and he later served as secretary of the Virginia colony. Thus Mark Catesby explained, "*Virginia* was the Place (as I had Relations there), which suited most with my Convenience to go to." He arrived in Williamsburg on April 23, 1712. Only a week later he met William Byrd II of Westover plantation, where Catesby spent three weeks beginning on May 24, 1712, taking walks with Byrd and helping him with his gardens. Catesby visited Westover many times as a guest and as a fellow naturalist and gardener.

In order to support his work in the New World, young Catesby, whom James Petiver called "that curious Botanist, . . . of Virginia," began to collect seeds and plant specimens to ship back to England. Catesby became acquainted with some of the leading botanists of the time, such as John Custis, during his sojourn in Virginia. He also traveled extensively, on one trip venturing westward into the Appalachian Mountains. During his trips Catesby kept voluminous notes and made drawings of flora and fauna. In 1714 Catesby went to Jamaica and Bermuda.

After staying in Virginia for seven years, in the autumn of 1719 Catesby sailed for England where he not only met with his patrons, people such as Sir Hans Sloane and William Sherard, but also with Colonel Francis Nicholson, who during his term as governor of South Carolina from 1720 to 1725 agreed to sponsor Catesby. The support of Nicholson and the Royal Society made possible Catesby's second trip to the New World. Catesby arrived in Charles Town in 1722 and immediately was introduced to some of the foremost families in that region. He made numerous trips to collect flora and fauna and sent seeds, plants, and animals back to his sponsors in England. In 1725 Catesby traveled to the Bahamas as a guest of George Phenney, the governor.

Catesby returned to England in 1726 and began the gigantic task of putting together his natural history. By the spring of 1729 he completed the first part of *The Natural History of Carolina, Florida and the Bahama Islands*, which was published in 1731. In order to produce the book and the plates as inexpensively as possible, Catesby not only colored the individual plates but also learned the engraving process and prepared the engravings himself. Eleven twenty-plate installments priced at two guineas each appeared. Eventually the plates were bound into the two volumes, the second of which was issued in 1743. In all, there were 220 plates illustrating 33 amphibians and reptiles, 31 insects, 9 quadrupeds, 171 plants, and most importantly, 113 birds on 109 plates. These plates, combined with descriptive text, presented a comprehensive illustrated natural history of America for the first time. As an added artistic dimension, animals and plants were illustrated on the same plates. On May 3, 1733, Mark Catesby was elected to membership in the Royal Society of London. He died in 1749, little knowing that his fame as a botanist would be totally surpassed by his ornithological achievements.

Naturalist and artist William Bartram (1739-1823) was the fifth son of John

Bartram (1699-1777), the self-taught Pennsylvania farmer who became America's first native botanist. In addition to being a naturalist, William Bartram was also quite interested in various aspects of the fauna of America. In his *Travels through North and South Carolina, Georgia, East and West Florida* (1791) he described in vivid detail not only plants and scenery but also animals and some birds and provided a catalog of 215 birds of the eastern United States, the fullest listing of American birds prior to that of Alexander Wilson (1766-1813). Wilson's *American Ornithology* (1808-1814) was such a prodigious achievement that it completely overshadowed any contribution to American ornithology that William Bartram made, and indeed Wilson should be credited as the "father of American ornithology." Yet Bartram's catalog paved the way for Wilson's monumental work.

Thomas Jefferson (1743-1826) was a naturalist in his own right. Jefferson's *Notes on the State of Virginia*, published in 1784, provided much valuable information on both flora and fauna and included a list of birds. Often cited as simply Thomas Jefferson's bird list, in reality it is Mark Catesby's list of birds, plus an additional three added by Jefferson.

Like his father, William Byrd II (1674-1744) was prominent in the affairs of the Virginia colony. Educated in England, Byrd was elected a fellow of the Royal Society at the age of twenty-one. After returning to Virginia, Byrd built Westover plantation on the banks of the James River and lived there for many years, maintaining particularly elegant gardens that many well-known people, including Mark Catesby, visited. A true servant of the crown, Byrd was a member of the House of Burgesses and then, for thirty-four years, of the governor's Council, serving as its president the year before his death in 1744.

William Byrd II wrote several books including *Histories of the Dividing Line Betwixt Virginia and North Carolina.* In 1737 he published a book that had been written in German and issued by a Swiss named Samuel Jenner entitled *Neu-gefundenes Eden* or "newly discovered Eden." Colonel Byrd had been trying to settle his "land of Eden" along the Roanoke River near the North Carolina border and had sold thirty-three thousand acres to Jenner. The book was intended as promotional material, and not until it was translated into English in 1940 as William Byrd's *Natural History of Virginia* was it discovered to be a plagiarism of John Lawson's *A New Voyage to Carolina*, originally published in 1709. John Brickell's *The Natural History of North Carolina* (1737) is another famous plagiarism of Lawson's book. The real author of *Natural History of Virginia* and *The Natural History of North Carolina* was Lawson and certainly not Byrd or Brickell.

The writings of John Lawson and Mark Catesby are of paramount importance for the study of natural history in the New World since the two men lived in North Carolina and Virginia, respectively, traveled throughout the colonial South, and were familiar with the birds in eighteenth-century Williamsburg.

# NORTHERN CARDINAL

*Cardinalis cardinalis*

"They are frequently brought from *Virginia*, and other parts of *North America*, for their beauty and agreeable singing; they having some notes not unlike our Nightingale, which in *England* seems to have caused its name of the *Virginia Nightingale*; though in those countries they call it the *Red Bird*." — MARK CATESBY

THE cardinal, the state bird of Virginia and North Carolina, is a very common permanent resident throughout the central and eastern United States where it occurs in almost all kinds of habitats except coastal swamps. The male is unmistakable, being a brilliant red all over with a cone-shaped reddish bill, a large red crest, and a black face. The female is a buffy olive brown with red on the crest, wings, and tail. The typical call of the cardinal, which has more than twenty different songs in its repertoire, is a clear *cheer, cheer, cheer* or *prety, prety, prety.*

Cardinals may fly through trees while foraging or hop about on the ground. They feed on virtually any type of beetle or other insect and are also quite fond of various kinds of seeds and fruit. Cardinals are easily attracted to feeders. Strongly territorial during the breeding season, they often fight with other males. The nest is placed five to ten feet above the ground; normally there are four eggs. Nests are frequently found in the boxwood hedges in the gardens of Colonial Williamsburg.

Among the best known species in colonial America, cardinals were popular cage birds. Lawson described the cardinal: "The Red-Birds (whose Cock is all over of a rich Scarlet Feather, with a tufted Crown on his Head, of the same Colour) are the Bigness of a Bunting-Lark, and very hardy, having a strong thick Bill. They will sing very prettily, when taken old, and put in a Cage. They are good Birds to turn a Cage with Bells; or if taught, as the Bulfinch is, I believe, would prove very docible."

# AMERICAN GOLDFINCH

*Carduelis tristis*

"They feed on Lettuce and Thistle seed. These Birds are not common in *Carolina*; in *Virginia* they are more frequent."
— MARK CATESBY

ALSO known as the "wild canary," American goldfinches are present at all times of the year in Virginia and North and South Carolina. Goldfinches are especially noticeable during the spring migration when large flocks often carpet the ground with their bright yellow hues. The males are remarkable for their brilliant canary yellow plumage, black wings, and black cap. Females are duller overall and lack the black cap. Winter birds of both sexes are a dull brownish yellow but retain the black pattern in their wings and tail.

The generic name *Carduelis* refers to thistle, and indeed it is appropriate because the goldfinches are intimately associated with and partial to that plant, using it for nesting materials as well as food. This species nests rather late after the thistle has bloomed. The nest is normally placed less than fifteen feet above the ground and usually contains five eggs. Goldfinches also eat a variety of seeds and are quite fond of sunflower seeds at feeders.

Goldfinches became one of the most popular cage birds, thriving well in captivity.

Two other finches that may be encountered in Williamsburg during the winter, particularly at feeders, are the purple finch *(Carpodacus purpureus)* and the house finch *(Carpodacus mexicanus)*. The males of both species are small, sparrowlike birds that have reddish or purple coloration and are streaked; the females are dull brown with dark streaks. Male purple finches have been described as a sparrow dipped in raspberry juice; they are a dull rosy red and are larger than house finches, which are smaller, brighter red birds. The females are also confusing, but purple finches are larger and have a broad, darkly colored jaw stripe.

Purple finches are native winter birds of the Williamsburg area, while house finches were introduced into the northeastern United States about 1940 and have rapidly spread their range.

Catesby painted the purple finch, noting, "When they first appear in *Carolina* (which is usually in *November)* they feed on the berries of Juniper; and in *February* they destroy the swelling buds of Fruit-Trees, in like manner as our Bull-finches do. They assemble in small flights, and retire at the approach of Winter." Lawson recorded the "Red Sparrow," which may have been the purple finch: "They are brown, and red, cinnamon Colour, striped."

# DARK-EYED JUNCO

*Junco hyemalis*

"In Virginia and Carolina they appear only in Winter; and in snow they appear most." — MARK CATESBY

THE dark-eyed junco (formerly slate-colored junco) is a common winter bird throughout Virginia and the Carolinas. It is encountered in greatest numbers from October to April when extreme cold and snow are present in the northern parts of its range. Catesby named this species the "Snow Bird" because the junco arrived in the winter when snow covered the ground. What a shame that his name did not carry through time! Lawson described the species: "The Snow-Birds are most numerous in the North Parts of *America*, where there are great Snows. They visit us sometimes in *Carolina*, when the Weather is harder than ordinary."

Dark-eyed juncos are small, sparrowlike birds with slate gray back upper parts — including the head and neck — white underparts, and white outer tail feathers. Some may be brownish gray. Juncos feed on the ground, generally scratching for their food, which consists primarily of small seeds. They often frequent bird feeders.

PRATT
1987

# INDIGO BUNTING

*Passerina cyanea*

"The *Spaniards* in *Mexico* call this Bird *Azul lexos,* or the far-fetch'd Blue-Bird." — MARK CATESBY

THE scientific name of these beautiful little blue finches, which provide a spot of welcome color in the countryside during the summer, is from the Latin *passer*, a sparrow, and the Greek *cyano*, meaning dark blue. Indigo buntings begin to arrive from their winter home in Central America about the middle of April and remain in this area until October.

The adult male is deep blue all over; the female is uniformly brown. The indigo bunting's song is a series of somewhat jumbled sounding high-pitched notes. Its close cousin, the spectacular painted bunting, a rare migrant in the Williamsburg area, is more often encountered to the south, especially along the coastal plain.

The indigo bunting prefers dry fields that are grown over in weeds but have some trees around the edges. It is also found along roadsides and in orchards. This species forages in bushy foliage as well as on the ground, consuming a variety of insects and seeds. The nest is normally placed in a small tree, sapling, or bush. Four eggs are the usual clutch.

The indigo bunting and the painted bunting were both popular cage birds. Catesby called the indigo bunting the "Blue Linnet." The painted bunting was commonly called the "nonpareil," and Catesby noted that "the *Spaniards* called this Bird *mariposa pintada,* or the painted Butterfly."

The blue grosbeak, a beautiful blue bird somewhat similar to the indigo bunting, may be found during the summer in farmed areas around Williamsburg. A larger, chunkier bird with a heavier bill and wide chestnut wing bars, the blue grosbeak typically perches in weeds near the ground, constantly twitching and spreading its tail. Like the female indigo bunting, the female blue grosbeak is a dull brown.

# RUFOUS-SIDED TOWHEE

*Pipilo erythrophthalmus*

"The Towhe Bird . . . is a solitary Bird; and one seldom sees them but in pairs. They breed and abide all the year . . . in the shadiest woods." — MARK CATESBY

ALSO known as the red-eyed towhee or "jorhee," this handsomely colored finch is a common permanent resident in most of the eastern United States. The male has black upper parts and a black hood and wings that meet its chestnut sides. The underparts are white. The female is similar in pattern to the male but substitutes brown parts for black. Named for its distinctive song, the towhee utters an emphatic *drink-your-teeee-ee*.

The rufous-sided towhee is a bird of dense undergrowth and thickets, although it may also be encountered in woodlands or residential areas. The towhee is most frequently seen perched, singing its melodious song, or on the ground scratching the undergrowth and leaves with both feet together. Its nest is usually placed in a low bush; normally four eggs are laid.

# EVENING GROSBEAK

*Coccothraustes vespertinus*

THE evening grosbeak is a large, stocky bird with a thick, conical bill. The male is mostly dull yellow with black wings that have large white patches; its tail is black. The female is silver gray with some yellow; her tail and wings are a dull version of the male's.

The evening grosbeak normally lives and nests in coniferous forests across the northern parts of Canada and the United States. It appears as a nomadic wanderer in small to moderate-sized flocks in the Williamsburg area only in the winter. How many grosbeaks visit the more southerly parts of the United States depends on the severity of the weather to the north; during particularly cold winters this species may be recorded in large numbers. In Virginia and the Carolinas the grosbeak feeds on the seeds of conifers as well as on buds and seeds of other trees. It is also quite fond of sunflower seeds, and huge flocks will descend on and devastate the contents of a well-stocked feeder.

Neither Lawson nor Catesby recorded the evening grosbeak. The species has expanded its winter range southward since the eighteenth century and was first recorded in Virginia and the Carolinas during the 1920s.

PRATT
1986

# MOURNING DOVE

*Zenaida macroura*

"Turtle Doves are here very plentiful; they devour the Pease; for which Reason, People make Traps and catch them."
— JOHN LAWSON

THIS species is Catesby's "Turtle of Carolina," which is common throughout the year in the eastern United States. In Virginia the nesting population is augmented by wintering migrants from the north. The mourning dove has the widest distribution of any North American game bird and is the only one that nests in all the original forty-eight states. Smaller than the domestic pigeon, it has a pointed rather than fan-shaped tail, the outer feathers of which are white. *Macroura* means mourning and refers to the mournful "cooing" note, a low-pitched *oowoo-woo-woo-woo* that is heard throughout the day during the breeding season.

Mourning doves are most often found in farm country where open grain fields are separated by rows of trees. They are also common in suburban areas where they nest near houses. The male brings twigs to the female at the nesting site, which is usually at a moderate height in the crotch of a tree. The flimsy nest accommodates two pure white eggs. Normally several broods are raised during a single breeding season. In the winter mourning doves live in small flocks near sites where food is plentiful and trees provide cover for roosting. Their diet is made up almost entirely of seeds of various types. Mourning doves are swift fliers that somewhat resemble hawks in flight. A characteristic whistling of the wings can be heard at some distance away as they fly.

The mourning dove was well known to early travelers in the New World, but little was written about the species because the larger passenger pigeon was so abundant.

# ROCK DOVE

*Columba livia*

PIGEON is derived from the Old French *pijon*, imitative of the piping of the nesting birds; dove is from the Dutch *duyve*, which subsequently became dove in Middle English. The names are used synonymously, although generally dove refers to the smaller members of the group, pigeon to the larger ones. Pigeons and doves are plump birds with broad chests and shoulders, small heads, and short necks. Their bills are thin and weak with a waxy-appearing cere at the base of the upper mandible that possesses slit-like nostrils. The thick plumage is sleek with many brilliant colors often in a "scaled" metallic or iridescent pattern.

The scientific name of the rock dove, *Columba*, is from the Latin for dove or pigeon; the Latin *livia*, blue gray, refers to its bluish plumage. The pure forms of this species that most closely approach its wild ancestor are essentially blue gray with a white rump and two black bars across each wing. The beautiful iridescent feathers on the head and neck reflect various hues of green, bronze, and purple. Through the centuries feather patterns, behavioral traits, and many color variants, ranging from pure white to an almost indescribable variety of colors, have been produced and are reflected in names such as pouter, carrier, runt, fan-tail, tumbler, frill-back, jacobin, and trumpeter, to mention only some of the main types.

Named for its preference in the wild state for constructing a flimsy nest of sticks and twigs on a rocky ledge, in the domesticated state the rock dove makes its nest on the ledge of an urban building or in the rafters of a barn. It lays two white eggs anytime during the year, most commonly in late spring to early summer or in the early fall. The food of the rock dove is diverse and consists mainly of grains of various kinds, berries, and insects. In cities the rock dove readily consumes bread and garbage.

Rock doves are thought to have been domesticated about 4500 B.C. and were used extensively as messengers by the Greeks and Romans. It is said that rock doves brought word of Caesar's conquest of Gaul to Rome; likewise, news of Napoleon's defeat at Waterloo first reached England by carrier pigeon. Homing pigeons are trained by gradually taking them farther and farther away from a home loft. They are able to return by using an accurate sun compass and their own internal clock, which compensates for the sun's movement. Homing pigeons may thus be trained to return from hundreds of miles away.

Rock doves were first introduced into the New World by the French at Port Royal, Nova Scotia, in 1606 and were brought to Virginia in 1621, so the rock dove has long been a familiar sight in Williamsburg. Numerous pigeon lofts where a soft gurgling *coo-roo-coo* is a familiar sound are located behind buildings in the Historic Area. During the colonial era nearly every farm had a pigeon loft. Much more elaborate structures known as dovecotes were also built as nesting sites for rock doves, which were considered a delicacy.

# YELLOW-BILLED CUCKOO

*Coccyzus americanus*

"It is a solitary Bird, frequenting the darkest recesses of woods and shady thickets." — MARK CATESBY

CATESBY'S "Cuckow of Carolina," one of the two species of cuckoos that occur in North America, is the one commonly seen in the middle and southern Atlantic states. The yellow-billed cuckoo arrives in April and remains until the end of October, leaving to spend the winter in South America. A rather nondescript bird, the yellow-billed cuckoo is easily recognized. It is grayish brown above (Alexander Wilson called this a "Quaker" color) and white below, with an exceptionally long tail that fans out somewhat in flight. The undertail is patterned strongly in bold black and white. Other features of recognition are the rufous wings and yellow lower mandible. Unlike other passerine birds that have three front and one hind toe, the cuckoo has a yoke-toed arrangement with two front and two hind toes.

Cuckoos are slow and deliberate and will remain motionless on a limb for several minutes, then suddenly fly to another tree. The yellow-billed cuckoo's characteristic and unmistakable call is a unique, guttural, staccato *kuk-kuk-kuk-kuk-kuk* ending in a retarded *koulp, koulp, koulp.* Although the call is uttered day after day throughout the summer, many people believe that it occurs only as a sign of approaching rain. According to Wilson, "in Virginia the *Rain-Crow* [is] observed to be most clamorous immediately before rain." When this colloquial name came into common usage is unknown, but it has become widespread across the southern United States.

John Lawson simply called it the "cuckoo": "The Cuckoo of *Carolina* may not properly be so call'd, because she never uses that Cry; yet she is of the same Bigness and Feather, and sucks the Small-Birds Eggs, as the *English* Cuckoo does." The practice of sucking other birds' eggs has been ascribed to the yellow-billed cuckoo throughout time and was mentioned by Wilson, but it is not known to have been observed.

The yellow-billed cuckoo is one of the most beneficial birds. One individual may consume immense quantities of insects in a day. Tent caterpillars are among its favorite foods, and over three hundred have been discovered in a single cuckoo's stomach. Cuckoos are also fond of beetles, wasps, dragonflies, and fruits such as mulberries and grapes. They even eat small frogs and lizards.

The yellow-billed cuckoo builds a flimsy nest of sticks and twigs in a small tree or shrub about ten to fifteen feet above the ground. Four blue green eggs constitute the normal clutch.

# RUBY-THROATED HUMMINGBIRD

*Archilochus colubris*

"The Humming-Bird is the Miracle of all our wing'd Animals."
— JOHN LAWSON

THE ruby-throated hummingbird arrives in mid-April from its wintering grounds in Mexico and Central America and remains until about mid-September, becoming widely distributed across the eastern two-thirds of the United States from southern Canada to Florida. It is the only species that nests in the eastern United States.

These unmistakable birds, a tiny three and three-quarter inches long, are a bright metallic green above with whitish underparts. The male is adorned with a brilliant red throat or gorget that appears to be black in poor lighting; the female lacks the red gorget. Also characteristic of this species are a twittering sound that is frequently uttered in flight, the buzzing of the rapidly beating wings, and a sharp *chip* while perched.

Since the more than three hundred species of hummingbirds are confined to the New World (where they are predominately tropical in distribution) they were a constant source of fascination to colonial naturalists, who had never encountered such a creature before. Catesby noted: "The Body is about the size of a Humble Bee . . . It receives its food from flowers, after the manner of Bees; its tongue being a tube, thru which it sucks the honey from them. It so poises itself by the quick hovering of its wings, that it seems without motion in the air."

The ruby-throated hummingbird is often encountered in the gardens of Colonial Williamsburg, performing its aerial antics as it flies forward and backward and hovers in front of flowers, its wings beating rapidly. Hummers are nectar feeders, and this particular species is strongly attracted to red, particularly flowers such as the trumpet creeper. Hummingbirds not only obtain the nutritious nectar but also eat tiny insects found about the flowers.

During migration hummingbirds feed in the blossoms of the dwarf flowering chestnut, or red buckeye. There are several buckeyes in Colonial Williamsburg gardens and near the East Wing of the Williamsburg Inn.

Ruby-throats build a remarkable nest, a walnut-sized structure of lichens and tiny bits of plant material that is bound together with spider webs and is placed in trees at moderate heights. Two pea-sized eggs are the normal clutch. During the breeding season hummingbirds often become quite aggressive and territorial, and they may attack and chase away other birds such as blue jays, crows, or even red-tailed hawks.

# NORTHERN BOBWHITE

*Colinus virginianus*

THE bobwhite or quail, Mark Catesby's "American Partridge," is a common resident species over most of the central and eastern United States and is quite abundant in the southeastern states. About half the size of a bantam, this chubby, chickenlike bird with a short tail is a mottled reddish brown. The male has a distinctive white throat and eye stripe that are buffy in the female. More frequently heard than seen, the voice is a clear *bob-white* or *bob-bob-white*, the last syllable being particularly loud and emphatic.

According to Lawson, "Our Partridges . . . often take upon Trees, and have a sort of Whistle and Call, quite different from those in *England*. They are a very beautiful Bird, and great Destroyers of the Pease in Plantations; wherefore, they set Traps, and catch many of them. These . . . arc less than the *European* Bird, but far finer Meat." Without question the bobwhite has been the South's most popular upland game bird since colonial days.

Except during the breeding season bobwhites feed and roost in coveys that range widely in brushlands, open woodlands, and farmlands that have enough hedgerows to provide adequate cover. When flushed, bobwhites rise swiftly with a loud whirring of beating wings, fly a short distance, put down, and begin walking or running with their characteristic bobbing motion.

Bobwhites' singing intensifies and they are seen more often when the breeding season arrives. The nest, placed on the ground and often shielded by a clump of grass or bushes, usually contains a clutch of twelve to eighteen eggs. After the young have fledged by late summer or early fall, families may group into coveys of as many as thirty birds. Toward roosting time they form several smaller groups that roost near each other on the ground, in circles, with their heads pointed outward. Such a configuration greatly conserves body heat, especially during the cold winter months. Catesby remarked that bobwhites "covy and roost on the branches of trees, frequenting woods and shady swamps more than open fields. Their flesh is remarkably white, and very delicate."

Wilson gave the first really extensive account of this species, noting that it was not at all uncommon, especially if the winter were harsh, for bobwhites to "mix with the poultry, to glean up a subsistence." Bobwhites have a tremendously varied diet, feeding on seeds of grasses, wild and cultivated grains, acorns, berries, grapes, dogwood berries, and persimmons.

# YELLOW-BELLIED SAPSUCKER

*Sphyrapicus varius*

THIS species is a common winter resident in the wooded sections of the South. Yellow-bellied sapsuckers nest from southeast Alaska south through the Rocky Mountains and much of southern Canada and the northern United States. They begin to arrive in the southern Atlantic states by late September and remain until early May, when they return to their breeding grounds.

The yellow-bellied sapsucker is a moderate-sized woodpecker that has a black back with whitish or buffy mottling and barring, a yellowish belly, a white rump, and large white wing patches. The head is black and white; the male has a red forecrown and a red chin.

The generic name for this bird is from the Greek *sphyra*, meaning a hammer or mallet, in reference to how it uses its bill to drill parallel rows of small holes in the bark of a tree, thereby allowing the sap to exude. The sapsucker returns to feed on the sap and the small insects that are attracted to it. It is doubtful that this practice actually causes the death of a tree, but many people feel that it damages its appearance. Fortunately the bird restricts its activity to only a small percentage of trees deemed commercially valuable, and it must be conceded that the sapsucker's beneficial value in controlling insects far outweighs any destructive tendencies it might have. Sapsucker holes can be seen in many trees in the Historic Area at Colonial Williamsburg.

The call note of the yellow-bellied sapsucker has been described as a nasal *cheer* slurring downward.

# RED-BELLIED WOODPECKER

*Melanerpes carolinus*

COLONIAL naturalists were usually quite astute when they chose descriptive names for America's birds, but in the case of the red-bellied woodpecker one has to search for the red belly, which is a slight wash of red on the lower underparts. This species has a beautiful black and white barred back with white upper tail feathers. The female has a red nape only, while the male sports a brilliant red crown and nape. The sides of the face and the underparts are gray.

A permanent common resident over the entire central and eastern United States, the red-bellied woodpecker is found in the residential areas of towns and small cities as well as in farmlands, orchards, and deciduous or mixed woodlands. It can often be seen in the Historic Area of Williamsburg.

This conspicuous woodpecker has been well known since colonial times for its depredations. Lawson described a woodpecker that was "a Plague to the Corn and Fruit; especially the Apples. He opens the Covering of the Young Corn, so that the Rain gets in, and rots it." The normal food of the red-bellied woodpecker includes caterpillars, beetles, the larvae of wood-boring insects, berries of various kinds, and wild grapes.

The call of the red-bellied woodpecker is a loud, querulous *chur-r-r-r-r-r*, which is similar to that of some tree frogs. During the breeding season this woodpecker is particularly noted for its drumming, which appears to serve to establish territorial dominance. It often chooses houses for this noisy ritual; drainage gutters are especially good for producing a loud, resonant sound.

PRATT
1987

# PILEATED WOODPECKER

*Dryocopus pileatus*

THE largest woodpecker in North America, the pileated wood-pecker measures seventeen inches. The only larger species is the ivory-billed woodpecker (twenty inches), which is now probably extinct but occurred in heavily forested bottomlands of the southern Atlantic states from southeast North Carolina southward. Also called the "Indian hen" or "log-god," the pileated woodpecker is found throughout the eastern United States as a resident species, although it is not particularly common any place in its range because this bird requires large expanses of woodland.

When perched, the pileated woodpecker appears almost entirely black on the back and wings. It has a white chin and white stripes on the head and neck. The male has a bright red head with a large red crest, while only the back part of the female's head is red. The bill is darkly colored. The call note is a loud, distinctive, and eruptive *kuk-kuk-kuk-kukkuk-kuk-kuk.*

This magnificent woodpecker occurs in both deciduous and conif-erous woodlands. While most frequently encountered in deeply wooded areas, it may also be found near human habitation. Its diet consists of approximately 75 percent animal and 25 percent vegetal matter. It can be heard pounding and chiseling at trees with its power-ful beak in search of wood-boring beetles and carpenter ants, which are among its favorite foods. It also eats other insects, wild cherries and grapes, acorns, and the seeds of sumac, poison ivy, and dogwood. The pileated woodpecker excavates its nest high up in a tree. The nest differs from those of other woodpeckers in being a rectangular or oval hole four inches or so in diameter.

Catesby described the "larger Red-crested Wood-pecker": "These birds . . . are destructive to Maiz, by pecking holes through the husks that inclose the grain, and letting in wet." Today the pileated wood-pecker is not reported to feed on corn.

# DOWNY WOODPECKER

*Picoides pubescens*

# HAIRY WOODPECKER

*Picoides villosus*

BOTH of these species range widely as permanent residents over the United States except for parts of the arid Southwest. The two are nearly identical in appearance, differing primarily in size, the downy being about six and three-quarters inches long, while the larger hairy measures nine and one-quarter inches. Each has a large white streak down the middle of the back, the remainder of which is black. The black wings are strongly striped and spotted with white; the underparts are solid white. There are two white stripes on the head, and the males have a red patch on the back of it. Hairy woodpeckers have longer, heavier bills and unmarked white outer tail feathers; downy woodpeckers have black markings on the outer white tail feathers. The call note of the downy is a soft *pik*, while the note of the hairy is a loud, sharp *peek.*

In the Williamsburg area the downy is the more common species of the two, inhabiting wooded groves, orchards, and swamplands. In general, the downy is more a bird of small branches and at times becomes quite acrobatic in its search for bark-dwelling insects. The hairy prefers dense forests and larger trees. Both species are frequently seen at bird feeders. The normal clutch is four to six eggs which are laid in nesting holes in stumps or dead limbs.

No one seems to know where the term hairy woodpecker comes from, since this species, like all other birds, has not a single hair on its body. Mark Catesby called the downy woodpecker the "smallest spot-

PRATT
1987

ted Wood-pecker" noting with respect to the hairy that "were it not for disparity of size, they might be thought to be the same." Lawson described a woodpecker as "black and white speckled, or mottled; the finest I ever saw. The Cock has a red Crown; he is not near so big as the others; . . . He is not very wild, but will let one come up to him, then shifts on the other side the Tree, from your sight; and so dodges you for a long time together."

# RED-HEADED WOODPECKER

*Melanerpes erythrocephalus*

"This is the only one of the Wood-peckers that may be termed *domestic*, frequenting villages and plantations, and taking a peculiar delight in rattling with its bill on the boarded houses." — MARK CATESBY

THIS handsome woodpecker is an uncommon permanent resident over its entire range, which includes the vast majority of central and eastern United States. Once much more common, the red-headed woodpecker has been greatly reduced in numbers because of the introduction in the 1890s of the European starling, a bird that competes vigorously with the red-head for nest holes. The red-head laboriously drills and excavates a nest hole in a tree, then the starling drives it away after persistent heckling. As a result, the woodpecker abandons one nest cavity after another until it ultimately fails to produce a brood. Although rare, the red-headed woodpecker may still be encountered in the Williamsburg area.

Many believe the red-head to be the most beautiful of the North American woodpeckers. It is easily identified by its solid red neck and head, blue black back, and snowy white underparts. In flight it exhibits white inner wing patches and a white rump. Like the other species of North American woodpeckers, the red-head has two hind and two front toes, a condition known as a zygodactyl or yoke-toed arrangement. Its long tongue is extensible and is equipped with sharp barbs for capturing insects. The stiff tail feathers with their spiny shafts aid in propping the red-head against the trunk of a tree.

The red-headed woodpecker often perches on old wooden posts, the trunks of large trees, or utility poles, darting out to catch flying insects. It also drills into tree trunks in pursuit of insects and forages on the ground for grubs, ants, and so on. The red-headed woodpecker consumes grapes, beechnuts, and acorns, which it sometimes stores. Occasionally it eats the eggs of bluebirds, chickadees, and titmice. The call of the red-head is a loud *queer, queer, queer.*

# NORTHERN FLICKER

*Colaptes auratus*

THIS species is usually known by the more descriptive name "yellow-hammer" or "yellow-shafted flicker"; Catesby called it the "Gold-wing'd Wood-pecker." The northern flicker occurs across the entire United States as a resident species and is common in the Williamsburg area. In the western states the yellow wing shafts become red, so a red-shafted flicker occurs west of the Rocky Mountains. Because yellow- and red-shafted flickers interbreed wherever they come into contact, the two are considered a single species.

The flicker is a large woodpecker, being nearly thirteen inches long. It has a brown barred back with a large white rump that is very conspicuous during its deeply undulating flight. There is a black patch across the chest and a red crescent on the nape; males have a black mustache. The underparts are conspicuously spotted with black dots. The song is a rapid *wik-wik-wik-wik-wik* and *wicker, wicker* or *flick-a, flick-a.*

The flicker is less strictly arboreal than other woodpeckers. Common in open woodlands as well as in suburban areas, the flicker is equally at home hitching up a tree trunk in typical woodpecker fashion or on the ground, where it hops around searching for ants, one of its favorite foods. Catesby noted that "it differs from other Wood-peckers in the . . . manner of feeding, which is usually on the ground, out of which it draws worms and other insects." He apparently mistook the bird's long extensible tongue for a worm!

# GREAT CRESTED FLYCATCHER

*Myiarchus crinitus*

"This Bird, by its ungrateful brawling noise, seems at variance, and displeased with all others." — MARK CATESBY

THE great crested flycatcher is found throughout the eastern United States in the summer, arriving from its wintering grounds in the northern and central parts of South America in April and not departing until September. It is a dark olive above, with a gray throat and breast and a lemon yellow belly. The dusky tail feathers exhibit extensive reddish color from the inner webs. A distinctive feature is the large bushy crest on the head. Equally characteristic of this species are its loud, mournful call, a descending *peeur,* and its rolling whistle, a *pree-pree-prreeit.*

The great crested flycatcher is a bird of the more open woodlands and may be found around farm woodlots, orchards, and in most wooded suburban areas. It sallies out from its perch in a tree to catch a great variety of insects on the wing, including dragonflies, beetles, bees, wasps, and flies of various kinds. The flycatcher also secures prey on the ground.

The crested flycatcher builds a nest of grasses, feathers, and other materials in a natural or man-made cavity. It lines the nest with a discarded snakeskin. No one knows why this bird chooses a snakeskin to adorn the perimeter of its nest, but one is invariably present. The snakeskin may serve to ward off natural enemies, or, like mud and horsehair, it may simply be a material that is used by the species.

PRATT
1987

# EASTERN KINGBIRD

*Tyrannus tyrannus*

"The courage of this little Bird is singular. He pursues and puts to flight all kinds of Birds that come near his station, from the smallest to the largest, none escaping his fury." — MARK CATESBY

THE eastern kingbird, whose scientific name comes from the Latin *Tyrannus*, meaning monarch or ruler, is a common summer resident over much of the United States except the extreme southwest. The kingbird arrives from its winter home in South America by early April and departs in late August and early September.

The kingbird has a black head, slate gray back with white underparts, and a white terminal band on the tail. An orange red crown patch usually is not visible. The bill is long and thick. It is a conspicuous, noisy bird whose frequent call is a harsh, high-pitched *tzi, tzee, tzi, tzee.*

The eastern kingbird frequents woodland clearings, fields, and orchards, often perching on fences or telephone lines along rural roads. It consumes huge quantities of various types of insects. Also called "field martin" or "bee martin," this bird has a decided preference for bees and has incurred the wrath of beekeepers for depredations on their hives.

While driving through the country in the summer, one frequently sees an eastern kingbird in pursuit of a crow, hawk, or other larger bird. The chances are twenty to one that the kingbird is on the attack, which is precisely the reason for its name. This species is absolutely fearless when it is defending its territory.

The nest, a substantial open structure of bark strips, twigs, or other plant material, can be found in a variety of places such as orchard trees or sycamores. The kingbird often builds near or over water.

Mark Catesby was fascinated with this species, which he termed "the tyrant." "I have seen one of them fix on the back of an Eagle, and persecute him, so that he has turned on his back into various postures in the air, in order to get rid of him, and at last was forced to alight on the top of the next tree, from whence he dared not move, till the little Tyrant was tired, or thought fit to leave him . . . the great ones, as Crows, Hawks, and Eagles, he won't suffer to come within a quarter of a mile of him without attacking them . . . When their young are flown, they are as peaceable as other Birds."

# BARN SWALLOW

*Hirundo rustica*

AMONG the most beloved of American birds, the barn swallow has been popular around farms since colonial times. The name comes from the Latin *hirundo*, swallow, and *rustica*, rural. Known in Europe simply as the swallow, this species is the most common summer resident swallow in the Williamsburg area. The barn swallow has a reddish breast, bluish back, reddish brown throat, and deeply forked tail. It feeds by catching insects on the wing.

Large flocks of migrating barn swallows arrive from their wintering grounds in South America by mid-March and disperse over the entire United States. Flocks begin to form for the return in July, and migration continues through September.

Early in the breeding season the male chases the female in long, involved courtship flights, uttering a constant twitter described as a *kvik-kvik*. The barn swallow prefers to nest in farm outbuildings such as barns but may also be found under eaves of houses or bridges and in cliffs or steep banks along lakes. The cup-shaped nest of clay pellets mixed with straw, feathers, and horsehair is affixed to the side of the appropriate site.

Catesby did not paint the barn swallow because it was such a common European species. Lawson simply noted: "Swallows, the same as in *England*."

# PURPLE MARTIN

*Progne subis*

"The Planters put Gourds on standing Poles, on purpose for these Fowl to build in, because they are a very Warlike Bird, and beat the Crows from the Plantations." — JOHN LAWSON

THE largest of the North American swallows, the purple martin is a popular summer resident over most of the central and eastern United States. In the springtime flocks of martins cross the Gulf of Mexico from their wintering rounds in South America, arriving in the Atlantic states by mid-March or early April. The return in the fall occurs over a long period with flocks coming together from late July to September.

The male martin is a dark glossy purplish blue all over; the female is purplish blue above and pale gray below. In flight the long wings and slightly forked tail are distinctive.

The Indians hung clusters of gourds, or calabashes, on poles to attract purple martins to nest in their villages. Colonial farmers carried on this practice since martins have traditionally been valued for their ability to ward off hawks from the chicken yard. Catesby wrote of the martin: "They breed like Pigeons, in lockers prepared for them against houses, and in gourds hung on poles for them to build in; they being of great use about houses and yards, for pursuing and chasing away Crows, Hawks, and other vermin, from the Poultry." Today elaborate houses are constructed for purple martins, and people throughout the South consider themselves fortunate to have a colony.

Special glazed earthenware bird bottles were used for purple martins in eighteenth-century Williamsburg. The 1746 inventory of tavern keeper John Burdett included "16 bird bottles." A number of archaeological sites, including the James Geddy property, have yielded fragments of the bird bottles, which are now being reproduced from their colonial prototypes. Other birds may have nested in the bottles (I have had bluebirds and Carolina wrens nest in mine), but they were surely designed for the purple martin.

Martins are extremely useful birds that consume great quantities of mosquitoes, dragonflies, wasps, and other flying insects.

# CHIMNEY SWIFT

*Chaetura pelagica*

THIS common species ranges widely during the summer over the entire central and eastern United States and southern Canada. Called by Catesby the "American Swallow" and Lawson "the Diveling," it is not a swallow at all but belongs to a unique family, the swifts, thought by many to be closely related to the hummingbirds.

The chimney swift has often been described as a cigar with wings, a description that is not too inaccurate. This blackish bird has long pointed wings and a squared-off tail with spines at the tips. The generic name is derived from the Greek *chaite*, stiff hair, and *oura*, tail, referring to the spiny tail characteristic of the species. While in flight the chimney swift utters loud chippering notes that are easily recognized.

Chimney swifts spend most of the day on the wing in constant pursuit of flying insects such as flies, mosquitoes, and beatles, which make up their entire diet. They wheel about in the sky, often at great heights, but may fly quite low to the ground, especially when the weather is cloudy or just after a rain. At dusk the swifts go to roost in chimneys, where they use their sharp claws to perch in the darkness, propping themselves against the vertical surfaces of the chimneys with the help of thin, stiff tails. The ends of the tail feathers are spiny.

Late in May chimney swifts break off small dead twigs and use their gluey saliva to build a nest on the inside of a chimney. The small semicircular basket accommodates three to six pure white eggs.

It is interesting to speculate about how the arrival of the first Europeans in America may have altered the habits of the chimney swift. Before the colonists built houses with chimneys, the birds depended entirely on large hollow trees for roosting and nesting sites. Audubon estimated that a massive hollow sycamore near Louisville, Kentucky, accommodated nine thousand roosting swifts, and Wilson said that when a large hollow beech was cut down it contained forty or fifty swifts' nests. Today, however, chimney swifts roost and nest almost exclusively in chimneys.

During spring migration large numbers of swifts roost in a chimney on Merchants Square in Williamsburg. Several hundred can be see swirling at sunset, and it is an impressive sight as they gather in loose circles that gradually tighten as they drop into the chimney to spend the night. Many stay through the summer, nesting in chimneys elsewhere in town.

Mark Catesby wrote an account of the American swallow in which he pointed out: "Their periodical retiring from, and returning to, *Virginia* and *Carolina,* is at the same seasons as our Swallows do in *England:* therefore the place they retire to from *Carolina* is, I think most probably *Brazil,* some part of which is in the same latitude in the Southern hemisphere, as Carolina is in the Northern; where, the seasons reverting, they may, by this alternate change, enjoy the year round an agreeable equality of climate." This is one of several places in his writings where Catesby showed considerable perspicuity concerning the then mysterious phenomenon of birds' migration. The chimney swift does make a lengthy migration, wintering mainly in northeastern Peru.

PRATT
1987

# BLUE JAY

*Cyanocitta cristata*

"Jays are here common, and very mischievous, in devouring our Fruit, and spoiling more than they eat. They are abundantly more beautiful, and finer feather'd than those in *Europe.*" — JOHN LAWSON

THE blue jay needs little introduction: with its beautiful blue back, white patches on otherwise blue wings, light gray underparts, and large blue crest, it is one of the most conspicuous birds in the middle and southern Atlantic states. This raucous bird is also well known for its call notes, a loud *jay, jay,* and the less frequently heard call that resembles a squeaky pump handle. A blue jay can imitate the red-tailed and other hawks.

Blue jays are found in almost any forest situation but seem to prefer more open woodlands, particularly those with mixed pine and oak. They are also permanent residents of America's towns and cities. Like the common crow — its close relative — the blue jay is omnivorous and consumes a great variety of both animal and vegetal food including nuts, berries, insects, frogs and other small vertebrates, and the eggs of other birds. Jays build bulky, loosely constructed nests high up in trees; three to five eggs form the normal clutch.

Catesby's painting of a scolding jay is considered one of his best illustrations of action, one reason why it was chosen for use in the Colonial Williamsburg film that features Catesby as *The Colonial Naturalist.* The transition from the artist's illustration to the live bird graphically demonstrates the quality of action that Catesby depicted in his painting.

One of Audubon's finest paintings is of three blue jays eating the eggs of another bird. He termed the blue jay a "rogue" and "thief," yet jays are tremendously helpful birds that consume large quantities of harmful insects and provide an image of unsurpassed beauty.

# AMERICAN CROW

*Corvus brachyrhynchos*

TWO species of crows, the American crow and the fish crow, occur commonly as permanent residents along the Atlantic seaboard. The American crow is by far the larger, more abundant, and more widespread of the two. If the birds are not seen together, however, it can be difficult to make a positive identification. The American crow is common throughout its range and occurs in a wide variety of habitats, but the fish crow is usually encountered near tidewater marshes. Perhaps the most reliable way of distinguishing between them is by their calls; the American crow utters the familiar *caw, caw,* while the fish crow has a distinctive, nasal, high-pitched *cah, cah.*

American crows are most conspicuous in the winter when they travel about in flocks. During the breeding season they tend to the duties of building the nest, a bulky structure of sticks and twigs lined with grasses, which is placed up to seventy-five feet high in a tree. Four to six olive green eggs are the usual clutch.

Crows are surely the most omnivorous of all birds, eating a great variety of insects, crustaceans, and small vertebrates and scavenging on carrion such as dead fish, road kills, and garbage. They also eat corn and other grain crops and can cause considerable damage. Crows are among the most intelligent birds and have been known to imitate human speech. They are capable of demonstrating learned behaviors such as flying up high with shellfish and then dropping them on rocks to break their shells.

Lawson wrote that "crows are here less than in *England.* They are as good Meat as a Pigeon; and never feed on any Carrion. They are great Enemies to the Corn-Fields; and cry and build almost like Rooks."

# CAROLINA CHICKADEE

*Parus carolinensis*

ONE of the most abundant birds at feeders during the winter, the Carolina chickadee is a common permanent resident of the southeastern United States woodlands. About five inches long, this diminutive bird is a dull gray all over and has a black cap and throat. As the Carolina chickadee moves through the woods, often in the company of other birds grouped together in small flocks, it continuously utters the distinctive call note, *chick-a-dee-dee-dee-dee.*

When the nesting season begins in early spring, these little birds become much noisier. Chickadees nest in tree cavities and will often take over a bird box if it is available. The normal clutch is five to eight eggs. After fledging the brood, the adults may often be seen feeding the baby chickadees lined up on a branch near the old nest site.

Although moths, caterpillars, bugs, beetles, and spiders compose nearly half of their food annually, seeds become a major part of the diet in the winter. Chickadees will make frequent trips to a feeder for sunflower seeds, each time flying off with a single seed that is broken open and then consumed.

Birds of this family are called "tits" in England. Catesby apparently did not feel it necessary to record this American species because of its general similarity to European forms.

# TUFTED TITMOUSE

*Parus bicolor*

PERMANENT common residents in Virginia and the southeastern United States, tufted titmice are the only other members of the family containing the titmice and chickadees that are found in the Williamsburg area. Titmice are easily identified by their appearance. They are small, slightly over six inches in total length, gray above and white below with a prominent pointed crest, blackish forehead, rusty brown flanks, and large, dark eyes. Their song is a very distinctive *peter, peter, peter.*

Tufted titmice are birds of deciduous and mixed woodlands. In the winter they commonly travel in small mixed foraging flocks of chickadees, kinglets, brown creepers, nuthatches, and other little birds. Like chickadees, titmice are primarily insectivorous during the summer. They are great acrobats, too, and forage hanging upside down while they glean small insects from the foliage. During the winter titmice often come to bird feeders for seeds or nuts, which they hold under their feet and crack open with blows from their bills.

Tufted titmice choose a natural cavity, bird box, or abandoned woodpecker nest for the nesting site, often lining it with a cast-off snakeskin as the crested flycatcher does. Five to eight eggs are the normal clutch.

Lawson referred to this species as "Tom-Tit, or Ox-Eyes, as in *England.*" Catesby painted the "crested Titmouse," which "breed in and inhabit *Virginia* and *Carolina* all the year. They do not frequent near houses, their abode being only amongst the forest trees; from which they get their food; which is Insects."

# WHITE-BREASTED NUTHATCH

*Sitta carolinensis*

# BROWN-HEADED NUTHATCH

*Sitta pusilla*

"The back claw is remarkably bigger and longer than the rest, which seems necessary to support their body in creeping down as well as up trees, in which action they are usually seen pecking their food, which is Insects, from the chinks or crevises of the bark." — MARK CATESBY

BOTH white-breasted and brown-headed nuthatches are common permanent residents of Virginia and the Carolinas. The white-breasted, the larger of the two, measures about six inches and has a blue gray back, white breast, and black cap; the flanks are tawny. The smaller brown-headed is only four and one-half inches long and is among the most diminutive birds. It is blue gray above, except for a buffy brown cap and nape, and has a spot of white in the brown of the nape where it meets the back. The lower parts are entirely white. The calls of these two species are very different: the white-breasted constantly utters a nasal *yank-yank-yank*; the brown-headed has a call described as a staccato *bit-bit-bit*.

Nuthatches are experts at creeping up and down trunks and limbs of trees, often head first, in pursuit of bark-dwelling insects such as beetles, bugs, moths, ants, spiders, and so forth. They will place a seed or nut in a crack in the bark and pound it with their beak until it breaks, hence the name "nuthatch," *hatch* being a corruption of *hack*. Both species come to feeders in the winter and are especially fond of sunflower seeds.

Primarily a bird of pine or mixed pine woodlands, the brown-headed nuthatch is not common in Williamsburg but can be found on

PRATT
1987

Jamestown Island. The white-breasted nuthatch prefers deciduous woodlands and may be encountered in the swamps and floodplains of the coastal region. Both species are cavity nesters. Catesby painted these two species of nuthatches together.

Another nuthatch species, the red-breasted, occurs as an uncommon migrant and winter visitor in the Williamsburg area. It is about the same size as the brown-headed but has a black cap with a white stripe over the eye, a black eye line, and is rust colored underneath.

PRATT
1987

# BROWN CREEPER

*Certhia familiaris*

THE brown creeper is the only New World member of the small Old World family that contains twelve species of creepers. Because this species occurs so widely in Europe, Catesby did not include it in his *Natural History*, nor is it mentioned by Lawson. In the Williamsburg area the brown creeper occurs only as a migrant species and winter resident from October to April.

This small bird, which is only slightly over five inches long, has white underparts and a pale rufous rump. Its streaked brown plumage camouflages the brown creeper somewhat when it perches on a tree trunk. The brown creeper's tail is exceptionally long for its size and is highly specialized for foraging on the trunks of trees: the spiny ends of the tail feathers help to prop the bird on the trunk. The brown creeper spirals upward along a tree, then flies to the base of another nearby and begins the process again; it does not move sideways and downward like a nuthatch. The call note of this species is a high-pitched *seee*.

Although insects and spiders found in the crevices of bark are the primary food of brown creepers, they also eat considerable quantities of seeds, especially in the winter. Pine seeds are a favorite. This species may be attracted to backyard feeding stations by suet rubbed into the bark of trees. They are very tame and become accustomed to human habitation; creepers have been known to alight on a man's leg during migration.

# CAROLINA WREN

*Thryothorus ludovicianus*

ALTHOUGH five species of wrens may be encountered at various times of the year in the Williamsburg area, the Carolina wren — so pervasive throughout the South — is the only common permanent resident. The largest of the wrens found in Williamsburg, the Carolina wren measures approximately five and a half inches. It is a rusty brown above and buff below, with a white throat and very prominent white eye stripe. A master vocalist, it enthusiastically repeats its loud, clear song that has been described as *tea-kettle, tea-kettle* or *cheery, cheery, cheery.* The Carolina wren sings at all times of the day and year.

Carolina wrens prefer shrubbery and tangles in yards and gardens, but they may also be found in isolated woods or swamps. They are always near the ground. These active little birds dart in and out of thickets as they pursue insects and spiders. They also eat small lizards and some berries and will come to bird feeders.

A pair of Carolina wrens may remain mated from one year to the next and sometimes return to the same nesting site for consecutive seasons. They are remarkable in their quest for unusual nesting places and have been known to select the absolutely most inconvenient site — a charcoal grill that has not yet been put to use for the summer, a work hat left in the garage, or a mailbox. Other, more natural locations are cavities in trees or stumps or abandoned woodpecker holes. Carolina wrens build a large, bulky, and partly domed nest of dead leaves, twigs, and rootlets and deposit from four to eight eggs.

Catesby did not record the Carolina wren. Lawson noted only that "the Wren is the same as in *Europe,* yet I never heard any Note she has in *Carolina.*"

PRATT
1987

# GOLDEN-CROWNED KINGLET

*Regulus satrapa*

# RUBY-CROWNED KINGLET

*Regulus calendula*

"In Winter Sun-shine days, they are wont to associate with other Creepers, particularly the Certhia, the Sitta, the Parus-ater . . . and other Tit-mice; ranging the Woods together, from tree to tree, as if they were all of one brood; running up and down the bark of lofty Oaks, from the crevises of which they collect their food, which are Insects lodged in their Winter dormitories, in a torpid state." — MARK CATESBY

THE two little North American kinglets that occur in the Williamsburg area are wayward members of the Old World warbler family. (A closely related form is the blue-gray gnatcatcher.) They arrive in eastern Virginia in October; the ruby-crowned, which is more common by far, remains until mid-May.

Kinglets are among the smallest North American songbirds, both species measuring four inches in length. Tiny and plump, they are grayish olive above, grayish white below, and have two white wing bars. The golden-crowned kinglet is distinguished by a white line over the eye that is bordered above by black. The male has a large orange crown patch bordered by yellow; the female's crown is yellow. The male ruby-crowned kinglet has a red crown patch that is seldom visible and is absent in the female; both sexes have a prominent white eye-ring. The call of the golden-crowned kinglet is a very high-pitched *ti-ti* or *tsee*, while that of the ruby-crowned kinglet is somewhat similar but is followed by descending *tew* notes.

The golden-crowned kinglet shows a decided preference for coniferous woodlands, whereas the ruby-crowned is more a bird of deciduous woodlands and thickets. They are nervous little birds that rapidly move about the foliage in their endless quest for small insects, spiders, and the like. The ruby-crowned constantly flicks its wings and often hovers at the tips of branches to secure small insects.

Catesby identified the kinglet as "an *English* as well as an *American* Bird," believing that it was the same species as the goldcrest *(Regulus regulus)* of England.

PRATT
1985

# BROWN THRASHER

*Toxostoma rufum*

"This bird is called in *Virginia* the *French Mock-Bird.* . . . It sings with some variety of notes, though not comparable to the Mock-bird." — Mark Catesby

THE brown thrasher is a common species in Virginia and the Carolinas during the summer months; it is less frequently seen in the winter. A large bird, about twelve inches in length, it is reddish brown above and pale buff below with heavily streaked underparts. This species is somewhat similar in coloration to the wood thrush, but the brown thrasher is a long bird, with a long tail and a long decurved bill.

Often erroneously referred to as the "brown thrush," the brown thrasher is not a thrush at all and, along with the catbird, is closely related to the mockingbird. All are in the family *Mimidae*, the mimic thrushes. The song of the brown thrasher resembles that of its cousin the mockingbird, but it is divided into spurts of two or three notes interrupted by slight pauses and the phrases are repeated. The brown thrasher may also mimic the cardinal, wood thrush, or titmouse.

Lawson viewed the brown thrasher as a second type of mockingbird: "There is another sort call'd the Ground-Mocking-Bird. She is the same bigness, and of a Cinnamon Colour. This Bird sings excellently well, but is not so common amongst us as the former." Catesby called this species the "Fox-coloured Thrush."

The brown thrasher has a decided preference for thick underbrush, hedgerows, and woodland edges close to human habitation. It forages on or near the ground, scratching the leaves beneath shrubs to uncover insects and grubs of various kinds. It also feeds on small snakes, lizards, and tree frogs and on wild fruits such as blackberries, holly berries, and hackberries. The nest is placed low in a bush near the ground. There are usually four or five eggs.

# GRAY CATBIRD

*Dumetella carolinensis*

"This Bird is not seen on lofty Trees, but frequents Bushes and Thickets; and feeds on Insects. It has but one note, which resembles the mewing of a Cat, and which has given it it's name." — MARK CATESBY

THE catbird is a common summer resident of Virginia and the Carolinas, and some individuals may remain throughout the winter. Dark gray all over, the catbird has a black cap, long black tail, and chestnut undertail feathers. The species is so named because of the nasal call note that resembles a catlike *mew*. A catbird sometimes mimics other birds and may have a number of musical phrases.

Although catbirds can be found in thickets and low-lying vegetation by the borders of marshes, roadsides, and the edges of forests, they seem to prefer bushes and gardens near human habitation where they forage close to the ground, frequently flicking their tails. Insects compose more than half of their diet. Other foods include wild and cultivated grapes and berries of all sorts. The nest is a deep cup of leaves, twigs, and grasses placed near the ground in the thick foliage of briers or similar plants. Four dark bluish green eggs are usual.

Lawson described "The Cat-Bird, so nam'd, because it makes a Noise exactly like young Cats. . . . They are no bigger than a Lark, yet will fight a Crow or any other great Bird."

PRATT
1985

# NORTHERN MOCKINGBIRD

*Mimus polyglottos*

"The *Indians*, by way of eminence of admiration, call it *Cencontlatolly*, or *four hundred tongues*; and we call it . . . the *Mock-Bird*, from its wonderful mocking and imitating the notes of all Birds, from the Humming Bird to the Eagle."
— MARK CATESBY

THE northern mockingbird, a common year-round species of suburban areas, barnyards, and pastures in the eastern and southern United States, defends its nesting and feeding territories very aggressively and constantly chases other birds away. A rather nondescript bird, it is dull gray above and paler below, with white wing patches and white outer tail feathers.

This bird is the most versatile songster in North America. Although the mockingbird has its own song, it is best known for imitating other birds. Its scientific name, *Mimus polyglottos*, "mimic of many tongues," is a true description of this species. A mockingbird may imitate birds as diverse as the red-tailed hawk and the blue jay and may even mimic artificial sounds such as bells or squeaky gates. One mockingbird was reported to be able to imitate the songs of more than fifty species of birds. Mockingbirds sing both day and night throughout the summer, especially when the moon is full.

Lawson called mockingbirds the "Choristers of *America*, . . . They sing with the greatest Diversity of Notes, that is possible for a Bird to change to. They may be bred up, and will sing with us tame in Cages; . . . They often sit upon our Chimneys in Summer, . . . and sing the whole Evening and most part of the Night."

A mockingbird frequently runs across a lawn flitting its wings, a distinctive habit known as "wing-flashing." Some observers believe that this action scares up flying insects, while others hypothesize that parents that have been on the nest are simply stretching their wings. Wing-flashing occurs in both breeding and nonbreeding seasons, and many who have watched carefully claim that no great number of insects seems to emerge, so the reason for this activity remains a mystery.

Insects and wild fruit compose most of the diet. The nest, which is usually built about ten feet above the ground, generally accommodates four to five eggs.

# WOOD THRUSH

*Hylocichla mustelina*

THE wood thrush is a fairly common summer resident in Virginia and the Carolinas from the coast to the lower and middle elevations in the mountains. The species usually returns from its wintering grounds in the tropics around April and remains until October.

Although a number of thrushes, including the eastern bluebird, hermit thrush, Swainson's thrush, gray-cheeked thrush, veery, and robin, occur in the Williamsburg area, the wood thrush is singular in appearance. It is a handsome reddish brown above, becoming brighter on the head, and white below, with large dark spots on the throat, breast, and sides and a distinctive white eye-ring. Often referred to as the nightingale, the wood thrush is best known for its song, a beautiful bell-like *ee-oh-lee, ee-oh-lay* that is repeated over and over. Many believe the wood thrush to have the most exquisite song of any North American bird.

Like most other thrushes (except the robin and bluebird) the wood thrush prefers areas that provide dense shade. Favorite habitats include moist deciduous or mixed woodlands, swamps, and undisturbed suburban low woodlands where the clear, flutelike song of this beautiful bird can be heard just before sundown in the summer.

The wood thrush is primarily insectivorous and feeds by catching beetles, ants, moths, flies, caterpillars, and spiders on or near the ground. It also consumes dogwood and Virginia creeper berries. The nest of the wood thrush is almost always located deep in the woods or in a swampy area, where it is placed near the ground. Three or four greenish blue eggs are the usual clutch.

Catesby did not paint or describe the wood thrush, but Lawson was aware of this species: "The Nightingales are different in Plumes from those in *Europe*. They always frequent the low Groves, where they sing very prettily all Night." George Edwards, the first to draw and engrave the wood thrush, based his illustrations on a bird that William Bartram sent to England.

# AMERICAN ROBIN

*Turdus migratorius*

THE American robin is one of the most familiar North American birds. Common summer residents in the Williamsburg area, robins are also present in smaller numbers throughout the year. The robins that spend the winter here usually migrate north to their breeding grounds and are replaced by others at the beginning of springtime; however, many birds that breed in a particular area will spend the entire winter if sufficient food is available. As a result, the movements of robins are erratic and unpredictable, the large spring migratory flocks giving the impression that they have arrived to signal the end of winter. Catesby called this bird the "Fieldfare of Carolina," commenting that "in Winter they arrive from the North in *Virginia* and *Carolina*, in numerous flights, and return in the spring as ours in *England*."

The American robin has a grayish brown back, brick red underparts, and a white lower belly. The dark head is almost black in some individuals; the white chin is streaked with black. Immature robins have speckled breasts. The American robin's well-known caroling has been described as *cheer-up, cheer, cheer, cheer-up.*

The American robin got its name from the first settlers, who thought it was similar to the European robin or "robin redbreast." The American species is much larger and has a brick red breast, while the European robin's breast is a pale orange red.

The American robin is well known for its consumption of earthworms. Berries and other wild fruits are also important in the diet. The robin's nest, a sturdy structure plastered together with large quantities of mud, is placed in the crotch of a tree about twenty feet or higher. Four "robin's-egg blue" eggs form the normal clutch.

PRATT
1985

# EASTERN BLUEBIRD

*Sialia sialis*

"A Blue-Bird is the exact Bigness of a Robin-red-breast. . . . Parts of him, are of as fine a Blue, as can possibly be seen in any thing in the World." — JOHN LAWSON

THE eastern bluebird is one of the most popular birds in the eastern United States where it occurs as a fairly common resident species. The male in breeding plumage is a bright blue above, with the breast and sides a reddish brown and the belly white. The female is paler and duller. The melodious song of the eastern bluebird is a soft *chur-lee* or *chur-wee*, which, once learned, is unmistakable.

Eastern bluebirds prefer open woodlands, farmyards, and wooded but open roadside areas. They are also found in urban settings where they have taken well to human habitation and are often seen on fences and utility lines.

Bluebirds are primarily insectivorous and frequently fly from a perch to the ground to catch a cricket or grasshopper. They are also fond of various kinds of berries — blackberries, bayberries, sumac, and Virginia creeper. Every year before the weather turns cold and we can enjoy the red pyracantha that covers the back side of our chimney, bluebirds devastate the berries. Then we lure them to our bird feeder by placing a combination of suet and clusters of sumac berries on it.

Bluebirds are early nesters, usually beginning their activities in March or sometimes even sooner. They build a simple nest, primarily of grasses, in the bottom of a natural cavity, a birdhouse, or other suitable place such as a mailbox. Normally bluebirds lay four pale blue eggs. They may raise several broods each year.

The bluebird has experienced a rather serious decline in recent years due largely to competition for nesting sites from the house sparrow and starling. Because so many people are now putting up bluebird houses, the species has recovered in a number of areas. Dr. T. E. Musselman of Quincy, Illinois, is credited with the innovative idea of establishing bluebird trails, a series of bluebird houses erected along country roads. In February 1935 he put up 102 houses along a forty-three-mile stretch of country road. As a result, bluebirds became a common sight in Adams County, Illinois, for the first time in twenty years.

The Williamsburg Bird Club has erected bluebird boxes along the Country Road to Carter's Grove plantation and at the plantation itself. Carolina chickadees, red-breasted nuthatches, and tufted titmice have also used the boxes.

PRATT
1987

# CEDAR WAXWING

*Bombycilla cedrorum*

THE cedar waxwing is an elegant little bird that appears in Virginia and the Carolinas primarily as a migrant and winter visitor. About the size of a bluebird, the cedar waxwing is a sleek brown with a conspicuous crest, yellow belly, and yellow band across the end of the tail. The most distinctive features are the black mask across the eyes and the red waxy tips on the ends of the secondary feathers of the wings that look like bright red sealing wax. Although Catesby called it the "chatterer," the cedar waxwing is among the most silent birds in this area. Its call is little more than a high wheezy whistle.

In the winter cedar waxwings traveling in small to large flocks consume huge quantities of berries, including those of such prized ornamentals as holly and pyracantha. They may gorge themselves until they can hardly fly. Occasionally a waxwing on the ground appears "drunk" from imbibing an excess of berry juice, but it is more likely that the berries have applied so much pressure to the blood vessels of the engorged bird's neck that it is temporarily incapacitated. Waxwings frequently invade the territory of a mockingbird in their quest for berries, and the poor mock-bird may spend the entire day chasing these rascals away from his yard.

# RED-EYED VIREO

*Vireo olivaceus*

THE species of vireos are restricted entirely to the New World. While not very conspicuous to the average observer, the red-eyed vireo is one of the most common summer residents of the central and eastern United States, arriving in Virginia and North and South Carolina in April and not departing until mid-October. It is a small, greenish, nondescript bird, about six inches in length, with a dark olive back and white underparts and a yellowish wash on the sides. The red-eyed vireo has a blue gray crown and a white eyebrow bordered above and below with black. It is difficult to see the red eye at a distance.

The song, a series of distinctive short phrases variously described as *here-I-am, where-are-you?* or *you-see-it, you-know-it, do-you-hear-me?* is a constant reminder of the red-eyed vireo's presence during the summer. It may be almost impossible to locate the bird after the trees leaf out, however.

The red-eyed vireo seems to prefer deciduous woodlands that are dry and somewhat open, foraging high in trees in a constant search for insects — beetles, caterpillars, moths, bees, and wasps. Large quantities of berries such as those of the Virginia creeper or blackberries are also consumed. The nest is a dainty pensile structure that may be as high as fifty feet above the ground. The normal clutch is four eggs.

Catesby called this species the "Red-ey'd Fly-catcher" and said that it "Weighs ten penny-weight and an half."

The white-eyed vireo also nests in this area. Olive green on the back with yellow sides and white below, the adult's white eye, yellow spectacles, and white wing bars are distinctive. The white-eyed vireo is more often heard than seen as it utters an explosive call that sounds like *whip, three cheers.*

PRATT
1987

# YELLOW-RUMPED WARBLER

*Dendroica coronata*

The "Yellow-rump . . . runs about the bodies of Trees, and feeds on Insects, which it pecks from the crevises of the bark." — MARK CATESBY

THE yellow-rumped warbler is a member of the New World family of wood warblers, the *Parulidae*, whose name comes from the Latin *parula*, a diminutive form of *parus*, or titmouse. These small birds have little relationship to the titmouse, however, and are probably more closely allied with the vireos. With their beautiful, often bizarre color patterns, the wood warblers, thirty-eight species of which occur in the Williamsburg area at one time or another of the year, have appropriately been termed the gems of the bird world. Because most of the wood warblers are transients, appearing briefly in the fall and spring, they were not well known to colonial naturalists. For example, Catesby painted and described only a handful of the North American species.

The yellow-rumped warbler is among the commonest winter residents in Virginia and the Carolinas from October to the beginning of May. A small bird (five and one-half inches), it has a yellow cap, yellow rump, and yellow patches on the sides of the breast. In the winter the yellow-rumped warbler has a brownish streaked back and whitish underparts with some streaking.

This active little bird feeds on small insects and a variety of plants, including the bayberry or myrtle, from which came its former name, myrtle warbler. It can often be observed in myrtle bushes. Yellow-rumped warblers occasionally visit bird feeders and will eat suet.

# RED-WINGED BLACKBIRD

*Agelaius phoeniceus*

CATESBY'S "red-wing'd Starling" is a common permanent resident in the Carolinas and Virginia. A frequently encountered nesting species during the summer, the population is greatly augmented in the fall and winter by a tremendous influx of migrants from the north.

This species is unmistakable. The male has a black body and red shoulder patches broadly tipped with yellow while the female is dark brown above and streaked below. The Latin name *phoeniceus*, meaning deep red, refers to the male's distinctive wing patches. The red-wing blackbird's song is a gurgling *konk-kee-ree* that is familiar to most people who enjoy the outdoors.

The scientific name for the genus comes from the Greek *agelaios*, of a flock, because of the conspicuous flocking behavior of red-wings in the winter, often in the company of other members of the blackbird family such as cowbirds and grackles. Huge flocks wing their way to feeding grounds during the day, returning at night to their roost, which may include incredible numbers of birds. One winter roost in the Great Dismal Swamp of Virginia was believed to contain fifteen million individuals.

Lawson noted that blackbirds are the "worst Vermine in *America*. They fly sometimes in such Flocks, that they destroy every thing before them." Catesby remarked that they "are most voracious corn-eaters. They seem . . . to do all the mischief they are able: and to make themselves most formidable, . . . committing their devastations all over the Country . . . They are the boldest and most destructive birds in the Country."

Red-wings feed on the ground on a great variety of weed seeds, waste grain, and other vegetable matter. They also eat insects, berries, and fruit, foods that are more important during the summer. After the winter flocks have dispersed in the springtime, red-wings pair for the purpose of nesting, often remaining in small groups that inhabit marshy areas with cattails, rushes, and the like. The nest is a woven cup of dried cattails or similar material fastened to marsh vegetation. The normal clutch is four pale blue eggs.

# COMMON GRACKLE

*Quiscalus quiscula*

THE word grackle originated in Europe where it was applied to members of the starling family. In the New World, however, grackle refers to the larger blackbirds that average about twelve inches in length and have long keel-shaped tails. Although tremendously variable in color, common grackles are predominantly glossy black. Birds from different geographical areas come in both "purple" and "bronze" varieties. Female grackles are smaller and duller than the males. Juveniles are brownish with brown eyes. As the adult plumage comes in, the eyes of common grackles change to yellow. They have a characteristic creaky call, a *koguba-leek*.

In the winter common grackles form large flocks with red-winged blackbirds, cowbirds, and starlings; during the summer they associate in small colonies for the purpose of nesting. Their bulky nests are placed fairly close together at moderate heights. Usually four to six eggs are laid. Comon grackles feed primarily in open fields where they walk about in pursuit of insects and caterpillars. During the winter they also eat seeds and waste grain.

Grackles, or "Purple Jack-Daw" as Catesby called them, have long been infamous for their depredations on grain crops: "In autumn, after a vast increase, they assemble together, and come amongst the inhabitants in such numbers that they sometimes darken the air, and are seen in continued flights for miles together, making great devastation of grain where they light. In winter they flock to barn doors. They have a rank smell; their flesh is coarse, black, and is seldom eat."

# EASTERN MEADOWLARK

*Sturnella magna*

"The Lark with us resorts to the Savannas, or natural Meads, and green Marshes. He is colour'd and heel'd as the Lark is; but his Breast is of a glittering fair Lemon-Colour, and he is as big as a Fieldfare." — JOHN LAWSON

THE eastern meadowlark, Catesby's "large Lark" or field lark as it is often called, is not a lark at all but a brightly colored member of the blackbird family. It is a common permanent resident throughout Virginia and the Carolinas. This ground-dwelling bird is predominantly streaked brown above with yellow underparts and a black V-shaped breast band. There is considerable variation in the intensity of the colors of the eastern meadowlark.

The song of the eastern meadowlark is a clear whistled series of notes variously interpreted as *see-you, see-yeer* or *tee-you, tee-air*, the last two notes being slurred downward. In its flight the meadowlark somewhat resembles the bobwhite, flapping quickly and then sailing for short distances on set wings.

Meadowlarks may be encountered in almost any country setting. They feed by walking around in grassy or weedy fields in search of the insects that account for about 75 percent of their diet, the remainder coming from seeds and grain. Meadowlarks nest on the ground. The usual clutch is five eggs.

Catesby described the meadowlark: "The breast has a large black mark, in form of a horse-shoe; except which, the throat and all the under parts of the body are yellow. It has a jetting motion with its tail."

# BROWN-HEADED COWBIRD

*Molothrus ater*

"In Winter they associate with the red wing'd Starling and purple Jack-daw in flights. They delight much to feed in the pens of cattle, which has given them their name." — MARK CATESBY

THE cowbird has apparently been extending its breeding range southward since the 1930s and can now be encountered fairly commonly in Virginia and the Carolinas any time of the year. The male cowbird is a metallic green black with a brown head; the female is a brown bird, paler below, with some streaking. The calls of the cowbird include squeaky whistles and a harsh rattling noise.

When speaking of cowbirds the term breeding rather then nesting must be used because these rogues do not bother to build a nest. Instead, the female simply lays her eggs in the nests of other birds. In other words, the cowbird is a brood parasite. The most frequently victimized birds in this area are the towhee, red-eyed vireo, and wood thrush. A cowbird usually lays one egg per nest of the host species. The cowbird chick grows faster than the others in the nest, much to their detriment. It crowds the nest and the other chicks cannot get their heads above the cowbird's so it is always fed first and invariably is the most successful nestling.

I once observed a fat cowbird chick on the ground beneath a large boxwood at Carter's Grove plantation. For over an hour, a song sparrow half the size of the cowbird chick struggled to satiate her adopted youngster by bringing it a large mouthful of grubs every few minutes.

Catesby called this species the "Cowpen Bird." As their name implies, cowbirds are often seen feeding around cows. They are fond of corn, wheat, seeds, and insects of all kinds.

# ORCHARD ORIOLE

*Icterus spurius*

## NORTHERN ORIOLE or BALTIMORE ORIOLE

*Icterus galbula*

"This gold-coloured Bird . . . is said to have its name from the Lord *Baltimore's* coat of arms." — MARK CATESBY

ORIOLES are brightly colored members of the New World blackbird family that are unrelated to the true orioles, which are songbirds of the Old World. The scientific name of the genus is derived from the Greek *ikteros*, meaning jaundice, an ancient name for a small yellow bird that was believed to cure a person with jaundice, after which the bird died.

Although closely related and placed in the same genus, the orchard oriole and northern oriole differ in their distributional patterns. The orchard oriole occurs in the summer in most of the central and eastern United States and is reasonably common in Virginia and the Carolinas, especially along the coastal plain. Although found over much of the United States as a summer bird, the northern oriole is a rather rare summer resident in the Williamsburg area. It is also a winter visitor, and during certain years flocks of a dozen or so may be seen at bird feeders.

The orchard oriole is tremendously variable in its plumages. An adult male is chestnut with a black hood, wings, and tail, while an adult female is olive above and greenish yellow below with two white wing bars. A first year male resembles the female but with somewhat darker colors and a black chin and throat. The Baltimore oriole is a bright orange bird with a black hood and upper back and a black tail with large orange patches on the outer feathers; the female is brownish olive above and dull orange below with blackish markings on her head. The orchard oriole has a song of whistled notes that are downslurred at the end, while the Baltimore oriole has more of a flutelike whistle. Both songs are difficult to describe.

The orchard oriole is abundant in groves and orchards. Insects comprise about 90 percent of this beneficial bird's diet; berries and fruit make up the remainder. It builds a carefully constructed woven pen-

dant nest that is placed about twenty feet above the ground. Four to six eggs are normal. The Baltimore oriole has a similar diet and builds a somewhat similar nest but prefers woodlands — extensive groves of trees along rivers, for example, or large shade trees in residential areas. People often put out old pieces of string and yarn for a Baltimore oriole to use in constructing its intricately woven nest.

The northern oriole was formerly called the Baltimore oriole, as Lawson explained: "The *Baltimore-Bird*, so call'd from the Lord *Baltimore*, Proprietor of all *Maryland*, in which Province many of them are found. They are the Bigness of a Linnet, with yellow Wings, and beautiful in other Colours." The species was actually named for its colors, which were those chosen by Sir George Calvert, the first Baron Baltimore, for his coat of arms. The "Baltimore" oriole hybridizes with its western relative, the "Bullock's" oriole, wherever they come into contact, so the two have consequently been placed in the same species. The compromise unfortunately involved dropping the name "Baltimore" and calling both the northern oriole. This is a ludicrous example of needlessly defiling history, and I urge readoption of the name Baltimore oriole for both eastern and western forms.

# SUMMER TANAGER

*Piranga rubra*

LIKE the wood warblers, the tanagers are members of a family that is restricted entirely to the New World and consists predominantly of species confined to tropical regions. Only four of the 160 or so species of this family reach the United States, and only two occur in the Williamsburg area. The summer tanager is the common summer resident in eastern Virginia and the Southeast, arriving in numbers in April and remaining until October. Catesby noted that "Summer Red-Birds . . . are Birds of Passage, leaving *Virginia* and *Carolina* in Winter."

Throughout the year the adult male is a bright rose red all over while the female is a light olive above and orange yellow below. A first spring male is a mottled mixture of green and red. The summer tanager is often confused with the somewhat similar scarlet tanager, which is less common locally. The male scarlet tanager is bright red with black wings; the female is olive green and also has black wings.

The call of the summer tanager is a staccato *chicky-tucky-tuck*, with the three phrases being repeated over and over. The call note is a loud series of *clucks.*

Summer tanagers are found almost anywhere there are woods but seem to prefer somewhat open, dry woodlands. Common in residential areas throughout the South, they are easily spotted as they move through the branches in quest of insects, including great numbers of bees and wasps. Summer tanagers also consume large quantities of blackberries, wild cherries, and such. They build a cup-shaped nest on a horizontal limb about twenty feet above the ground. Four eggs are usually laid.

Some compare the summer tanager and the scarlet tanager with the cardinal, but tanagers do not have a crest like the cardinal does.

# COMMON NIGHTHAWK

*Chordeiles minor*

THE generic name of this species, *Chordeiles*, comes from *chorde*, the Greek word for a stringed musical instrument; *deile*, afternoon or evening, refers to the nighthawk's loud calls during the evening hours. While it is not a hawk at all, the common nighthawk does "hawk" insects on the wing. Unlike its cousins the whip-poor-will and chuck-will's-widow, it is frequently seen during the day.

The common nighthawk has long, pointed wings and a slightly forked tail. It is gray or grayish brown and is easily distinguished by the bold white wing bars that are visible near the wing tips in flight. Nighthawks actively pursue insects in a darting flight, often with erratic beats of their wings. Flying sometimes low, sometimes high over roofs or fields, they continuously utter their characteristic loud *peent* call which, once heard, can never be confused.

The common nighthawk occurs over the entire United States and southern Canada and extends into Mexico. Prodigious numbers are seen during the August and April migrations, with some flocks numbering over one thousand individuals. Nighthawks spend the winter in South America.

These strange birds have intrigued naturalists since colonial times. John Lawson knew this species as the mosquito hawk: "*East-India* Bats or Musqueto Hawks, are the Bigness of a Cuckoo, and much of the same Colour. They are so call'd, because the same sort is found in the *East-Indies*. They appear only in the Summer, and live on Flies, which they catch in the Air, as Gnats, Musquetos, etc." Catesby totally confused the species in this group and his "Goat-sucker of Carolina" has many features of a nighthawk, including the white wing bars. "In the evening they appear most, and especially in cloudy weather: before rain, the air is full of them . . . they make a hollow and surprizing noise; which to strangers is very observable, especially at dusk of the evening, when the cause is not to be seen. This noise is like that made by the wind blowing into a hollow vessel; wherefore I conceive it is occasion'd by their wide mouth forcibly opposing the air."

The common nighthawk was well known in early America. In Louisiana the French Creoles called it the "crapaud volant"; in Virginia it was simply the "bat." The best-known name for the species in the South today is still "bullbat." American Indians commonly used onomatopes of birds' calls for their names, so the common nighthawk was called "peesk" by the Hudson Bay Indians and "besh-que" by the Chippewa, who surprisingly distinguished it from the whip-poor-will, to which they gave the sonic name "gwen-og-wi-a."

One reason why the common nighthawk was so familiar is its remarkable courtship flight that occurs during the breeding season. The male performs a spectacular aerial display, rising to a great height, then suddenly diving down with wings and tail half closed toward the female on the ground. Just as a crash appears inevitable, the male brakes by stretching out his wings and expanding his tail and then turns upward abruptly. The wind rushing through his wing feathers produces a loud booming sound.

# CHUCK-WILL'S-WIDOW

*Caprimulgus carolinensis*

MARK Catesby's "Goat-sucker of Carolina" was a combination of the chuck-will's-widow and the common nighthawk. He appears to have been totally confused by these strange "ghosts of the night" known as goatsuckers or nightjars. The origin of Catesby's name dates back to ancient times in rural Europe, where these large-mouthed, batlike birds fed at dusk on the wing, flying in and around pastures, and were thought to pilfer milk from grazing goats.

Goatsuckers in the eastern United States include this nocturnal species and the whip-poor-will, as well as the more diurnal common nighthawk. The chuck-will's-widow, common in the summer throughout the southeastern United States, is the largest nightjar. It is a mottled buff brown all over and has rounded wings and a long rounded tail. The male has a white neck band as well as some white in his tail feathers. The smaller whip-poor-will occurs as an uncommon migrant in Williamsburg. It may nest here and is found in rural areas nearby. The whip-poor-will is mottled gray brown all over and has considerable white in its tail.

During the spring and summer months the chuck is the common bird along the coastal plain, especially in pine woods; it is less frequent or is transient in the Piedmont and mountains, where the whip is more prevalent. There is some overlap, however. Colonial naturalists clearly did not distinguish between the chuck and the whip, so comments about the whip-poor-will probably really refer to the chuck since it predominates in the areas in which Catesby and Lawson lived.

The chuck returns to tidewater Virginia by the latter part of April and begins its nightly ritual, the woods resounding with the loud resonant echo *chuck-will-widow*, which is normally repeated six or eight times at intervals of about two and one-half seconds. Sometimes an individual emits an astonishing number of repetitions; over eight hundred in succession have been reported!

With an enormous mouth that is about two inches wide, the chuck has an incredible appetite and feeds almost exclusively on the wing, capturing flying beetles, moths, and other insects as well as an occasional small bird such as a wren or sparrow. Chucks are normally seen flying along the edges of woods and fields in pursuit of insects, often uttering an eerie growl, *cluck*, or *chuck*.

Catesby's confusion over the nightjars is apparent in a letter to John Bartram in 1741: "There is a bird in Virginia . . . that at night calls *Whipper Will*, and, sometimes, *Whip Will's widow*, by which names it is called (as the bird clinketh, the fool thinketh) . . . I believe it is a kind of cuckoo."

In his account of the whip, which undoubtedly refers to the chuck, Catesby stated: "The Indians say these Birds were never known till a great massacre was made of their countryfolks by the *English*, and that they are the souls of departed spirits of the massacred Indians. Abundance of people here look upon them as birds of ill omen, and are very melancholy if one of them happens to light upon their house, or near their door, and set up his cry (as they will sometimes upon the very threshold) for they verily believe one of the family will die very soon after."

# CHIPPING SPARROW

*Spizella passerina*

ALTHOUGH chipping sparrows occur in Virginia and the Carolinas throughout the year, they are most commonly encountered as breeding birds during the summer. About five and a half inches long, these small sparrows are brown streaked with black and rust above and gray below. Breeding adults may be identified by the bright chestnut crown, broad white eyebrow, and black line from the bill to the back of the head. Outside of the breeding season the head becomes buffy gray with streaks. Chipping sparrows derive their name from their conspicuous trill of *chip* notes, all on approximately the same pitch.

These charming little birds are among the smallest and tamest of the many species of sparrows in the Williamsburg area. They are found in a great variety of habitats, including edges of woodlands, fields, and grassy lawns. Chipping sparrows are quite common around human habitation and will come up to a porch if fed bread crumbs over a period of time. They have even been known to take food from one's hand. Normally chipping sparrows feed on the ground, scratching continuously for small weed seeds or similar food. They are also fond of various kinds of small insects.

Chipping sparrows build a nest of grasses and weed stems on the ground, in bushes, or in trees as high as thirty feet. They usually include hairs — preferably from horses — in the nest and sometimes take hairs from sleeping dogs. They have been called "hairbirds" for this reason. Three to five eggs are the normal clutch; two or three broods are raised per year. After breeding, chipping sparrows form small flocks, often in the company of pine warblers and other species of sparrows.

Song sparrows can also be heard and seen in the gardens of Colonial Williamsburg. They are rather drab with heavily streaked underparts and a large central spot on their breasts. The song, which is repeated frequently, consists of three short notes followed by a trill.

# WHITE-THROATED SPARROW

*Zonotrichia albicollis*

WHITE-THROATED sparrows nest throughout much of southern Canada and the extreme northeastern United States and then migrate south to spend the winter. They are among the commonest winter birds across most of the eastern and southeastern United States.

These birds are brown above with considerable streaking and have whitish gray underparts and a white belly. They also have a conspicuous white throat, dark stripes on the crown, a dark eye line, and a yellow spot between the eye and the bill. As spring approaches, white-throated sparrows begin to acquire their nuptial plumage and the head stripes change to black, with white in between.

Various attempts have been made to represent the white-throat's song in words. Perhaps the most popular comes from New England where it is called the "peabody bird" because it sings *Old Sam Peabody, Peabody, Peabody.* During the winter a frequently uttered slurred *tseet* and a sharp *chink* are often heard.

White-throated sparrows arrive in late September or early October and congregate in small groups or — more often — in larger flocks until the latter part of April or May, when they depart for their breeding grounds. They are fond of almost any kind of bushy area or low-lying shrubbery where they feed on the ground, scratching the underbrush for seeds of various kinds. White-throated sparrows are common birds at feeders.

Colonial naturalists were not particularly keen on the sparrow family. To them, these small birds were similar to the dull sparrows of England and were hardly worthy of mention. Lawson noted, "Sparrows here differ in Feather from the *English.* We have several Species of Birds call'd Sparrows."

PRATT
1987

# KILLDEER

*Charadrius vociferus*

"In Virginia they are called kill-deers, from some resemblance of their noise to the sound of that word." — MARK CATESBY

BOTH the scientific name, *vociferus*, and the common name, killdeer, refer to the loud, persistent call of this species, which is repeated time after time at the slightest alarm. In fact, killdeer is a phonetic approximation of the first call, *kill-deeah*, which is repeated along with a *dee-dee-dee.* Equally distinctive are the double black chest bands displayed over the otherwise white underparts and the reddish rump that appears in flight.

The killdeer, or "Chattering Plover," as Catesby called it, may be the best known and most widely distributed North American shorebird. It is the common resident plover of the southern Atlantic coastal states, where it occurs inland as well as along the coast. Unlike most shorebirds, the killdeer is fond of pastures, meadows, and even cultivated fields. It may also be found along shores and riverbanks. Usually seen in pairs or small flocks, the killdeer alternately runs and stands in its pursuit of food, which consists of about 98 percent insects. Some seeds are also eaten.

Nesting usually begins in May, when killdeers seem to become much noiser and more conspicuous. They are skilled actors during the breeding season and will feign a broken wing or leg in a noisy, acrobatic fashion while leading an intruder away from the nest. The alarm and anxiety exhibited by these birds during the breeding season are remarkable; their cries may often be heard long after dusk and well before dawn.

Killdeers do not attempt to hide the nest, which is no more than a shallow depression in the ground lined with grasses or a few pebbles. The usual clutch is four buffy eggs splotched with chocolate brown. Upon hatching, the downy young have a pattern that bears a strong resemblance to the adults'. Almost as soon as they are out of the egg and their feathers are dry, they begin to run about on the ground with their parents.

John Lawson recorded the species: "The Lap-wing or Green-Plover are here very common. They cry pretty much, as the *English* Plovers do; and differ not much in Feather, but want a third of their Bigness." Catesby stated that "these Birds are very frequent both in *Virginia* and *Carolina*; and are a great hinderance to Fowlers, by alarming the game with their screaming noise." Wilson noted at the turn of the eighteenth century that in the planters' yards in South Carolina the "negro boys frequently practice the barbarous mode of catching them with a line, at the extremity of which is a crooked pin, with a worm on it."

# WILD TURKEY

*Meleagris gallopavo*

"The wild Turkeys of *America* much excel the *European* tame breed, in stature, shape, and beauty of their plumage."
— MARK CATESBY

THE wild turkey is the most unusual North American bird and has become almost as much a symbol of the United States as the bald eagle. The wild turkey is a sleek version of the barnyard fowl. Its naked bluish head has long red wattles, and its body is a beautiful bronzy iridescent color. Males have a black beard of modified hairlike feathers. The call of the wild turkey is identical to the familiar gobbling of the domesticated variety.

Like the eagle, the wild turkey has unfortunately become greatly diminished in numbers over much of its former range. While once very common in the Williamsburg area, it now must be listed as an uncommon resident species of the deeply wooded, remote regions of Virginia.

The wild turkey was a major item in the diets of both the Indians and the early colonists. The Indians also held it in high esteem for adornment and used the cocks' spurs as arrow points. There is no evidence that the Indians of eastern North America attempted to domesticate the wild turkey before the first Europeans arrived. The turkey was a common domesticated fowl of the Mexican Aztecs, however. Early accounts of the species were written in 1519 by Hernando Cortez, who is thought to have been the first to take turkeys back to Europe where they spread rapidly. Brought back to America from the Old World, domesticated wild turkeys became a common fowl in colonial America as well.

John Lawson, who traveled extensively throughout North Carolina, observed great numbers of turkeys, stating in 1709 that "I have seen about five hundred in a Flock." Lawson indicated that wild birds sometimes bred with tame ones: "I have been inform'd, that if you take these wild Eggs, when just on the point of being hatch'd, and dip them (for some small time) in a Bowl of Milk-warm Water, it will take off their wild Nature, and make them as tame and domestick as the others."

It is unfortunate that Catesby did not paint the American wild turkey or write an account of the species, presumably because the domesticated turkey was such a common fowl in Europe. That Catesby neglected this species is even more interesting when one considers that Benjamin Franklin vehemently spoke out against the bald eagle and in favor of the wild turkey as our national emblem. Franklin argued that the turkey was "a true original native of America." Later, Audubon chose the wild turkey as the symbol for his monumental *Birds of America*, in which he lamented the choice of the eagle instead of the wild turkey.

# WOOD DUCK

*Aix sponsa*

COMMON throughout this region, the wood duck or summer duck is the most beautiful species of North American waterfowl. The Latin name is derived from the Greek *aix*, meaning a water bird, and the Latin *sponsa*, a bride or "promised one," in reference to the male's exquisite plumage, as though ready for betrothal.

Although they are much less common in winter, wood ducks can be found throughout the year in freshwater swamps, wooded ponds, and river bottoms, particularly in the eastern parts of Virginia and North and South Carolina. The male is a resplendent bird, his neck and breast a rich burgundy spotted with white, golden flanks, and a remarkable dark green slicked-back crest and head accented with a scarlet red eye, white throat, and variegated bill patterned in red, yellow, black, and white. The female is a nondescript brown bird with a white teardrop eyespot on a gray brown crested head. Wood ducks have a distinctive call note, a squealing *hoo-eek* or *oo-eek*.

Wood ducks have always been very popular game birds whose flesh is considered to be among the best of the waterfowl. This is presumably due to their diet, which is devoid of fish and consists to a large extent of acorns, water hickory nuts, duckweed, and aquatic seeds of various kinds. Vegetable matter is thought to comprise over 90 percent of their total food intake.

With the exception of the hooded merganser, the wood duck is the only duck native to Virginia that builds its nest in a tree cavity, which may be in the abandoned roosting site of a pileated woodpecker. Lawson noted that the wood duck builds its nest "in a Wood-pecker's Hole, very often sixty or seventy Foot high."

One of Catesby's best paintings is of the summer duck, a species that intrigued him because of its nesting habits. "They breed in *Virginia* and *Carolina*, and make their nests in the holes of tall trees (made by Wood-peckers) growing in water, particularly cypress trees. While they are young, and unable to fly, the old ones carry them on their back from their nests into the water; and at the approach of danger, they fix with their bills on the backs of the old ones, which fly away with them."

There has long been a debate as to how the young get to the ground after they hatch. Most reliable reports indicate that they jump, and it is interesting that those young raised in captivity must be dropped from a height of six feet or so into a tank of water before they will proceed to take their food. During the colonial period wood ducks were often domesticated as adornments for the yard, and they were shipped to Europe for the same purpose. Alexander Wilson wrote that "among other gaudy feathers which the Indians ornament the calumet or pipe of peace, the skin of the head and neck of the Summer Duck is frequently seen covering the stem."

Wood ducks nesting in a tree on the campus of the College of William and Mary brought traffic to a halt as they crossed a busy thoroughfare heading for the nearest water, the newly hatched ducklings following the female.

# BUFFLEHEAD

*Bucephala albeola*

THE little bufflehead is one of the more spectacular waterfowl of this region. It is a fairly frequent migrant and winter resident in Virginia from November to April or May. Buffleheads are more abundant along the coast than inland but can be seen with some regularity in small flocks of up to forty or so on the larger lakes and rivers.

The bufflehead is a very distinctive miniature duck. The male is mostly white and has a dark greenish head with a large white patch extending across the back from eye to eye. The legs and feet are a bright pink. The dull female shows much less white and her dark head is marked only by an elongate white spot just beneath the eye. The generic name *Bucephala* comes from the Greek meaning Buffalo-headed, a reference to the large-headed appearance of the male.

Like the scaup, the bufflehead is a "diving duck." They often dive for food in small groups, with one or more individuals remaining on the surface to keep watch for danger. Their food consists of both plant and animal matter and may include small fish, aquatic insects, snails, shrimp, crustaceans, and seeds of pondweeds of various kinds. The diet varies considerably depending on whether the species is in fresh or salt water. During the main migration in October and November these little ducks get so fat that the hunters find them quite easy to decoy; the colloquial name "butterball" is applied at this time.

Mark Catesby was quite familiar with this species, which he termed the "Buffel's-Head Duck." He described the male and female as two distinct species, calling the female the "little brown duck." He said that males were found on "fresh waters, and appear in *Carolina* only in Winter" while females "frequent the lower parts of rivers in *Carolina*, where the water is salt, or brackish."

The ruddy duck is another small common duck that is found in many of the same areas as the bufflehead. In the winter both species can be easily spotted from the Colonial Parkway, which winds along the York River toward Yorktown.

PRATT
1985

# MALLARD

*Anas platyrhynchos*

PERHAPS the best known of all the North American ducks, the mallard is a common migrant and winter resident in the southern Atlantic states, where it can be found in a great variety of freshwater habitats throughout the region. The male is readily identified by his green head and neck, which contrast with the large yellow bill. A narrow white collar separates the neck from the chestnut breast. The female is a mottled brown. Mallards have been extensively domesticated since colonial times and are therefore common in parks, aviaries, and barnyards. The name is derived from the Old French *maslard*, meaning wild drake.

Because the mallard may be the most abundant wild duck in the temperate regions of the world and is a common domesticated variety in Europe — it is, in fact, the ancestor of all of the breeds of domestic ducks except for the Mexican muscovy — Mark Catesby paid little attention to it in his *Natural History*.

Lawson, who was less concerned with repeating species that occurred in Europe, did list the mallard: "We have of the same Ducks, and Mallards with green Heads, in great Flocks. They are accounted the coarsest sort of our Water-Fowl." Other sources, however, indicate that in America as in Europe, the mallard was considered among the best ducks for eating, both for the flavor of the meat and for the large size of the birds.

Mallards and wood ducks are known as "dabbling ducks." They are also called pond or puddle ducks because they usually feed in shallow water lakes and ponds where they obtain food by tipping up and "dabbling." Most of their diet consists of vegetable material that they can reach by simply upending. Mallards feed on seeds of the bulrush, primrose willow, wild rice, and pondweed that are obtained at depths of a foot or two although they may dive deeper when necessary. In contrast, ducks such as the scaup and bufflehead are "diving ducks" and normally descend to thirty feet or more in pursuit of aquatic plants or fish.

Domesticated mallards may be seen on the Governor's Palace canal.

# LESSER SCAUP

*Aythya affinis*

THE lesser scaup, a winter visitor from October to May, is one of the most abundant ducks in the southern Atlantic and Gulf states during migration. It is called scaup because it feeds on shellfish. The name comes from "scalp," or shell, and refers to "mussel-scalps" or "muscle-scaups," the beds of rock or sand to which mussels cling. The lesser scaup has a gray back with whitish sides and a dark purple head and breast glossed with green. Lesser scaup form huge rafts that are often seen on large freshwater rivers and lakes.

The lesser scaup is an expert diver and swims rapidly under water with its webbed feet, often diving to feed at depths of five to six feet. Like other "diving" ducks, however, it may descend to twenty feet or more in its pursuit of small aquatic insects, which constitute about half of its diet. Scaups eat an equal amount of plant food, including pondweeds, widgeon grass, and wild rice.

Catesby did not record the species because scaups were well known in England. Lawson noted: "Raft-Fowl includes all the sorts of small Ducks and Teal, that go in Rafts along the Shoar, and are of several sorts, that we know by no Name for." Scaups have been hunted intensely since colonial times and are still a popular game fowl; they swim low in the water and are not easily taken. If wounded, scaups normally do not fly but may dive to great depths to escape, often reappearing as far as thirty yards or so from the original site.

The greater scaup, a very similar species, is somewhat larger and is normally found along the coast on salt water, rarely appearing inland. A less common but similar winter bird is the ring-necked duck, which has a black back instead of the silver gray of the scaup and a black-tipped blue bill with a distinct white band separating the black from the blue.

PRATT
1985

# GREAT BLUE HERON

*Ardea herodias*

THE great blue heron, also known simply as the great heron, is the largest, best known, and most widespread of all the North American members of the family *Ardeidae*, which contains species that fly with their necks pulled back on their shoulders in an S-shaped fashion. Mark Catesby called this bird the "largest crested Heron" and noted that "they are natives of Virginia." Country folk have tended to call all herons — and especially this species — cranes, and the name blue crane is often heard. However, the only true cranes in North America are the sandhill crane and the whooping crane, large birds that fly with their necks outstretched like geese and are not found in this area.

The great blue heron is a large slate blue bird that is nearly four feet tall. It has a long sharp-pointed yellowish bill and a white head with a black stripe extending above the eye. The call note has been described as a raucous *frahnk, frahnk.*

Great blues range widely over North America from southern Canada to Mexico and may spend the winter in northern South America. They are common permanent residents in Virginia where they occur either singly or in small groups. They inhabit the coastal regions in both fresh- and saltwater situations, nesting in undisturbed wooded swamps. Great blue herons become somewhat rare inland in the summer. If the snow is deep in the winter, they seek the clear areas of cedar and cypress swamps.

These majestic herons can frequently be seen standing alone and motionless on a pond or lake. When great blues take flight, they often utter their characteristic call, flying with large, slowly beating wings, their long legs trailing behind. Their primary food consists of fish, although they also eat frogs, lizards, snakes, insects, and even small birds and mice. Although great blue herons feed by both night and day, they are most active at dawn and just before dusk.

Herons are not eaten today, but during the eighteenth century and later great blues were considered a delicacy "when properly cooked," and their young were said to be excellent for the table.

From the colonial period to the turn of the twentieth century, herons and egrets were slaughtered for their plumes, which become greatly exaggerated during the breeding season. Some species were endangered from about 1840 until around 1900, but thanks to protection fostered by the National Audubon Society most have recovered.

A number of other herons occur, although less commonly, in and around Williamsburg. Rarely seen in the summer, great and snowy egrets are occasional visitors during the fall and spring. The little blue heron is also an uncommon transient that is rarely encountered during the summer. Great and snowy egrets and first year little blue herons are solid white birds that can be spotted at a great distance. Catesby described the immature "white" little blue as a species distinct from the adult.

# GREEN-BACKED HERON

*Butorides striatus*

"They . . . sit . . . on trees hanging over rivers, in a lonely manner, waiting for their prey, which is Frogs, Crabs, and other small Fish." — MARK CATESBY

THIS small crow-sized heron is the most common heron during the summer months and can be found on virtually every pond, brook, and lake across the South. Some of the names by which the green-backed heron is known are "Indian hen," "fly-up-the-creek," and "shitepoke." Catesby called it the "Small Bittern" and stated that "I don't remember to have seen any of them in Winter; therefore I believe they retire from Virginia and Carolina more South."

The green-backed heron is easily recognized as a small, chunky heron with short yellow orange legs. The back and upper parts of the adult are a dark green mixed with blue gray; the neck is a deep chestnut with greenish black feathers on the crown that are raised like a crest.

The green-backed heron is at home in both salt- and freshwater habitats where it is normally seen singly or in pairs along streams and ponds that have wooded cover. It wades stealthily in the shallows along the shoreline, crouched, head and neck pointed forward. Suddenly spotting its prey, the green-backed heron strikes quickly and skillfully, seldom missing. Its diet consists of small fish, frogs, crayfish, insects, small snakes, and mice. When alarmed, the green-backed heron raises its dark green crest and flicks its tail nervously. The green-backed heron invariably utters a characteristic *show* or *sheow* while flying.

Green-backed herons usually nest as single pairs in a slough or near a pond. The stick nest is placed ten to fifteen feet above the ground. After the breeding season this species may remain until the latter part of October; by April they are again present throughout Virginia. A common bird of the marshes along the country road to Carter's Grove plantation, green-backs can also be seen fishing in the canal at the Governor's Palace.

# CANADA GOOSE

*Branta canadensis*

THE Canada goose, which is familiar to nearly all Americans, is the common wild goose. The regular periodic migrations of this magnificent bird herald the approaching cold winter, and it is difficult to imagine that anyone is not familiar with the V-shaped flocks of these geese, honking as they travel southward in the fall.

The large Canada goose is easily recognized by its black head and black neck that is marked with a distinctive white chin strap, or, as Catesby described it, "a white stay or muffler." The characteristic honking call note has been variously described as *ah-honk* or *ka-ronk*, with a slight break in the middle of the two syllables.

The Canada goose was especially common during colonial times and was esteemed both as food and as a domesticated barnyard fowl. In the New World, domesticated Canada geese were used as live decoys on hunting trips, a practice that resulted in great numbers of wild geese being shot. Wounded wild Canada geese were frequently placed with domesticated geese with which they bred. Canada geese were also transported to England and France where they became popular as a domesticated variety. In his account of this species, the French naturalist Georges Louis Leclerc de Buffon (1707-1788) noted that hundreds of Canada geese inhabited the great canal at Versailles, where they bred with the swans.

When Canada geese migrate south for the winter, they are most common along the Atlantic Coast, although they sometimes occur inland in the eastern part of Virginia and the Carolinas. During the past several decades they have been attracted to the Eastern Shore of Maryland because the area is cultivated with crops such as wheat, corn, and soybeans that they find easily accessible, inducing most of the geese to remain there for the entire winter. Consequently, they have become much less numerous farther south.

Canada geese feed on vegetable matter including aquatic plants, seeds, and roots and tubers of various kinds. They are strong grazers and will eat not only wild vegetation but also freshly sprouted winter wheat, corn, and rice, a habit that has made them unpopular with farmers. Geese normally feed in the early morning and late afternoon and spend the day resting on open water or on sandbars and mudflats.

Geese are among the few birds that mate for life, and the family does not normally break up at the end of the breeding season as is true of most birds. Instead, the parents and young may remain together for almost a year and migrate north together in the springtime.

The smaller snow goose and blue goose, now considered to be color phases of the same species, *Chen caerulescens*, because of extensive hybridization, are regularly found in the winter — although in small numbers — at Hog Island State Refuge opposite Jamestown. These geese are either solid white with black wing tips or brownish gray with a white head and neck and black wing tips.

PRATT
1985

# LAUGHING GULL

*Larus atricilla*

"We have a great pied Gull, black and white, which seems to have a black Hood on his Head." — JOHN LAWSON

ALSO known as the black-headed gull, this species is easily recognized by its distinctive red bill, black hood, and dark slate gray upper surfaces. The neck and underparts are white. During the nonbreeding season the bill turns black and the head may become grayish with some white mixed in. Aside from its appearance, the laughing gull is also identified by its laughing note, *ha, ha, ha, ha, haah, haah, haah.* Catesby remarked, "The noise they make has some resemblance to laughing, from which they seem to take their name."

This gull is well known to residents of the Atlantic coastal states as the beggar of ferry passengers and fishing boats, gleaning the refuse of fishermen. Virtually any morsel of food, especially bread, tossed overboard is immediately caught by a hungry gull that often grabs the tidbit while it is in the air. Very common along the coast, laughing gulls in numbers also venture inland up rivers such as the James, where they follow the ferries that cross back and forth from Jamestown to Scotland Wharf.

In its normal habitat the laughing gull catches small fish that swim near the surface and even alights on the head of a brown pelican to take food from its pouch. It eats earthworms from freshly plowed or flooded fields and takes the eggs and downy young of terns. Laughing gulls nest in colonies along the coast in grassy saltwater marshes. Their well-constructed nests typically contain four eggs.

The laughing gull was the only gull that Catesby recorded in his *Natural History,* no doubt in part because he was mainly interested in birds that were both unique to North America and spectacular.

One of the most conspicuous winter gulls on the James River today is the greater black-backed gull, another species that has appeared in the past thirty years. It previously lived only in the far north but now is common in this area. However, the common winter gull is the ring-billed, which arrives in the winter as the laughing gull migrates south.

# SORA

*Porzana carolina*

"These Birds become so very fat in Autumn, by feeding on Wild Oats, that they can't escape the *Indians*, who catch abundance by running them down. In *Virginia* . . . they are as much in request for the delicacy of their flesh, as the Rice-Bird is in *Carolina*."
— Mark Catesby

THE sora, or "Soree" as Catesby called it, is a rail, a bird of wet marshlands that is much more often heard than seen. In fact, soras are normally spotted only when they come out to feed by the edge of a marsh. They step daintily over lily pads or floating pieces of vegetation or wade in shallow waters, picking up bits of food here and there while continuously flitting their short tails up and down. If alarmed, the sora's body narrows incredibly and it is able to slip through stalks of grass or reeds that are quite close together, hence the expression "thin as a rail." Soras may also swim across narrow channels of water.

"Sora" is the Indian name for this species in Virginia. Soras are chubby birds with bright yellow chickenlike bills. The adults, which are olive above and gray below with white streaks, have a black area around the base of the yellow bill and throat. The primary call is a *ker-wee* followed by a descending *whinny.*

Soras breed widely across the southern parts of Canada and the northern half of the United States but are only transients over much of the South, including Virginia, where Catesby encountered them. They appear in the southern Atlantic states in great numbers during the fall migration, when they may occur in almost any type of marshy situation, both fresh- and saltwater, as well as wet, grassy fields. In the fall soras feed on a variety of insects and aquatic vegetation such as smartweed and the leaves of duckweed; they are particularly fond of wild rice. During their migrations, enormous groups may concentrate in areas where wild or cultivated rice is present.

Because soras have a heavy layer of fat beneath their skin, they have been eagerly sought by hunters. Wilson said that soras occurred in "prodigious" numbers in Virginia particularly along the shores of the James River. He told of killing five with one discharge of his shotgun and said that it was not uncommon "for an active hunter to kill ten or twelve dozen in a tide." At night hunters used a canoe rigged with a sort of mast that had a fire atop on a grate. The birds, appearing astonished at the light, were struck down with paddles. "Twenty to eighty dozens have been killed by three negros, in the space of three hours" in this manner.

Soras are noted for their extreme clumsiness in flight. They seem to fly only as a last resort, and when they do, it is a very weak flight for only a short distance. Yet these mysterious birds undertake great migrations, returning with precision to their nesting grounds each year. The soras disappear when the first frosts occur along the Altantic coast; in Virginia, it was commonly thought that they burrowed into the mud. Another theory was that the soras turned into frogs, an idea that gained credence because the frogs ceased to holler when the soras arrived in the fall.

# BELTED KINGFISHER

*Megaceryle alcyon*

THE belted kingfisher is a stocky bird, about thirteen inches long, with short legs and a large head that has a ragged crest and an oversized bill. It is blue gray above with white neck and white underparts. The female has a rust belly band and flanks. The kingfisher utters a loud, rattling *rickety, crick, crick, crick* that is unmistakable. The ancient Greeks called the kingfisher *halkyon* (halcyon) in the belief that it nested in the open sea and that the gods so favored the species that they calmed the waters during nesting time.

The belted kingfisher ranges widely over most of the United States as a resident species and is the only kingfisher north of Texas and Arizona. In this region Lawson's "little Dipper or Fisher" is found by lakes, rivers, and ponds where it perches conspicuously on a limb, watching for prey. The kingfisher eats mainly small fish that it catches by diving into the water, often disappearing beneath the surface temporarily. It also consumes tadpoles, crayfishes, lizards, frogs, and small snakes. "Its cry, its solitary abode about rivers, and its manner of feeding, are much the same as of those in *England*. It preys not only on Fish, but likewise on Lizards," wrote Catesby.

A kingfisher's nest may occasionally be encountered in the summer. It is a horizontal burrow dug into the bank of a stream or lake, often extending three to seven feet in length. Kingfishers are notoriously poor housekeepers and their nests have an exceptionally foul odor.

# OSPREY

*Pandion haliaetus*

"The Fishing-Hawk is the Eagle's Jackal, which most commonly
. . . takes his Prey for him." — JOHN LAWSON

THE osprey, or "fishing hawk," is one of the most widely distributed birds, occurring over most of the Old World as well as North America. In the southern Atlantic states ospreys are uncommon and very local inland but are found with some regularity in coastal areas, particularly during the summer months. They have been recorded nesting along the York and James rivers.

This spectacular species is dark brown above and white below with a white head exhibiting a prominent dark eye stripe. In flight the characteristic long, narrow wings are bent back slightly at the wrist, superficially similar to those of gulls. The osprey resembles the bald eagle in its general appearance but is smaller and its underparts are white instead of black.

Ospreys normally nest along coastal regions, inland lakes, and rivers in tall dead trees near their feeding areas. They build a large, bulky structure of sticks that somewhat resembles the bald eagle's. Like eagles, ospreys use and enlarge the same nest year after year.

The osprey is a fisherman par excellence. Its feet, which have specialized, deeply curved, sharp claws and toes that are profusely covered with sharp spicules on the pads, are peculiarly adapted for grasping slippery fish, the osprey's main food. Its diet consists almost exclusively of live bluefish, catfish, flounder, perch, pike, and suckers. The osprey flies from thirty to one hundred feet above the surface seeking its prey. When a fish is sighted, the osprey hovers, wings beating, and then dives with a large splash, emerging with its prize, which is taken back to the perch in a dead tree for dissection. An osprey always carries fish — which may weigh four pounds or more — parallel to its body, the head of the fish pointing forward.

Lawson and Catesby were both intrigued by the pirating relationship of the bald eagle to the osprey, Lawson stating that the osprey is "the most dexterous Fowl in Nature at Catching of Fish, which he wholly lives on, never eating any Flesh." Catesby recorded that the osprey's "manner of fishing is, after hovering a while over the water, to precipitate into it with prodigious swiftness; where it remains for some minutes, and seldom rises without a fish; which the Bald Eagle, which is generally on the watch, no sooner spies, but at him furiously he flies; the Hawk mounts, screaming out, but the Eagle always soars above him, and compels the Hawk to let it fall; which the Eagle seldom fails of catching, before it reaches the water. It is remarkable, that whenever the Hawk catches a fish, he calls, as if it were, for the Eagle; who always obeys the call, if within hearing."

# RED-TAILED HAWK

*Buteo jamaicensis*

THE red-tailed hawk is among the best known and most widely distributed of the North American hawks and may have a wider habitat tolerance than any other hawk. The red-tailed hawk is a "buteo" hawk. Known throughout the Old World as buzzards, these hawks with broad wings are highly adept at soaring and are therefore most frequently seen on outstretched wings high overhead, tracing broad circles in pursuit of prey.

This species is easily recognized as a large-bodied hawk with broad, rounded wings and wide tail that is often fanned. The plumage is highly variable, but these birds are basically dark brown above and white below with brown streaks on the lower neck and a broad band of streaking across the otherwise white belly. Most, although not all, adults have a red tail; normally the young have a banded tail that may require three years to become red. The red-tailed hawk has a distinctive call, a harsh descending *kree-e-e-e*, often uttered while on wing.

This species unfortunately acquired the name chicken hawk because of its occasional depredations on the poultry yard. As a consequence, the red-tailed hawk has been persecuted over the years. In reality, the red-tailed hawk is enormously beneficial to farmers. Most of its food consists of small rodents, snakes, lizards, squirrels, rabbits, muskrats, skunks, and carrion. Occasionally poultry is eaten, but certainly no more than 7 percent of the diet is so composed. Furthermore, the red-tailed hawk is most likely to take old and diseased or very young birds and thus in the long run may even help to improve the chicken yard.

The red-tailed hawk is a fairly common permanent resident of the southern Atlantic states, normally nesting in April. During the fall the population is greatly augmented by migrants from the north that spend the entire winter in the area, when the red-tailed hawk becomes most conspicuous. It is the large hawk seen along roadsides in trees and on telephone poles or soaring overhead. The preferred habitat in Virginia is mixed country — open pastures and farm fields interspersed with woods.

PRATT
1987

# AMERICAN KESTREL

*Falco sparverius*

THE American kestrel or sparrow hawk is the smallest and most common of the North American falcons. The species name, *sparverius*, is from the French *espervier*, sparrow hawk, which is really a misnomer since this species is not a true hawk and sparrows constitute only a small portion of its diet.

The kestrel is widely distributed in the southern Atlantic states. It becomes very common in the winter but less so during the breeding season when much of the population migrates to the north to breed. The American kestrel is easily identified by its russet back and tail and the double black stripes on its white face. Males have blue gray wings.

American kestrels are most often seen perched on wires along roadsides. They raise and lower their tails repeatedly while keeping an eye out for possible prey. Although normally found in open and farm country, kestrels may also frequent towns and cities. Their diet consists of insects of all kinds, mice, small birds, small snakes and lizards, and even bats and frogs. While hunting kestrels fly with rapid wingbeats over open country, gliding occasionally. They often stop in midair, hover with rapidly beating wings, and then descend to the ground to grasp the prey in their talons, wings partly folded. They return to the perch to eat. When kestrels are alarmed they often utter a *killy-killy-killy*, from which the local name of "killy-hawk" is derived.

Lawson said that the kestrel "flies at the Bush and sometimes kills a small Bird, but his chiefest Food is Reptiles, as Beetles, Grashoppers, and such small things." "The Little Hawk," wrote Catesby, "weighs three ounces and sixteen penny weight. . . . They abide all the year in *Virginia* . . . preying not only on small birds, but Mice, Lizards, Beetles, etc."

PRATT
1986

# BALD EAGLE

*Haliaeetus leucocephalus*

"The Eagle is reckon'd the King of Birds." — JOHN LAWSON

THE magnificent bald eagle, or "White-Headed Eagle" as Mark Catesby called it, is a real treat to see. The adult, which has a wing span of more than six feet, is dark brown except for a white head and tail. Young birds are brown all over and are irregularly marked with white until about the fourth year, when the adult plumage is complete. When eagles soar, their huge wings are held straight so that the outer primaries appear individually.

The bald eagle is a rare resident species in eastern Virginia. Some years ago they were reported to be nesting in the Newport News city park and the Jamestown area. During the winter bald eagles can sometimes be seen along the James and York rivers, particularly if the weather has been severe enough to freeze rivers farther north, which forces them to migrate south in search of open water where fish are available.

The bald eagle was abundant along the Atlantic coast during the colonial period. John White drew it, and both Lawson and Catesby wrote detailed accounts of this species, Lawson noting that "this Eagle is not bald, till he is one or two years old."

A powerful and stately bird, the bald eagle has served as the national emblem of the United States since June 20, 1782. Its choice was not without controversy. Benjamin Franklin, for example, strongly opposed selecting the eagle: "Others object to the *bald eagle* as looking too much like a *dindon*, or turkey. For my own part, I wish the bald eagle had not been chosen as the representative of our country; he is a bird of bad moral character; . . . For in truth, the turkey is in comparison a much more respectable bird, and withal a true original native of America. Eagles have been found in all countries, but the turkey was peculiar to ours; . . . He is, besides (though a little vain and silly, it is true, but not the worse emblem for that,) a bird of courage, and would not hesitate to attack a grenadier of the British guard, who should presume to invade his farmyard with a *red* coat on."

John James Audubon later lamented the choice of the eagle: "Suffer me, kind reader, to say how much I grieve that it should have been selected as the Emblem of my Country." But why such concern over choosing the stately eagle as the symbol of the power and majesty of this great new land? The answer lies in the bald eagle's propensity for eating carrion – its main source of food – which usually consists of dead fish picked up along the shore! But the bald eagle will also consume dead lambs

and calves, a habit that has been to its detriment since most farmers believe that it was responsible for killing the animals. The truth is that an eagle rarely kills small farm animals.

Eighteenth-century writers inaccurately recorded the eagle's feeding habits, Catesby stating that it "has great strength and spirit, preying on pigs, lambs, and fawns." He did not mention fish. Lawson noted that the eagle "is an excellent Artist at stealing young Pigs, which Prey he carries alive to his Nest, at which time the poor Pig makes such a Noise over Head, that Strangers that have heard them cry, and not seen the Bird and his Prey, have thought there were Flying Sows and Pigs in that Country." He also observed that the bald eagle took fish away from the osprey: "They are heavy of Flight, and cannot get their Food by Swiftness, to help which there is a Fishawk that catches Fishes, and suffers the Eagle to take them from her, although she is long-wing'd and a swift Flyer, and can make far better way in her Flight than the Eagle can."

The nest, which is usually placed in a large tree such as a cypress, is the biggest built by a single pair of birds in North America: it may be up to eight feet across and twelve feet deep. Eagles mate for life and add to their nest year after year. Catesby wrote, "They always make their Nests near the sea, or great rivers, and usually on old dead Pine or Cypress-trees, continuing to build annually on the same tree, til it falls."

Catesby did not like the name bald eagle, preferring, as did Audubon later, white-headed eagle: "This bird is called the Bald Eagle, both in *Virginia* and *Carolina*, though his head is as much feather'd as the other parts of his body."

The Bald Eagle by Mark Catesby.

# TURKEY VULTURE

*Cathartes aura*

"The Turkey-Buzzard of *Carolina* is a small Vulture, which lives on any dead Carcasses. They are about the Bigness of the Fishing-Hawk, and have a nasty Smell with them. They . . . are reported to be an Enemy to Snakes, by killing all they meet withal of that Kind." — JOHN LAWSON

FEW people during colonial times were aware that two species of vultures existed side by side over much of the continent. Most Americans today also believe that only one type presides over the carrion of the countryside. Yet both the turkey vulture, or "Turkey Buzzard" as Catesby called it, and the black vulture, or carrion crow, may be seen with some regularity.

The turkey vulture is a gentle glider, rocking from side to side in flight and seldom flapping its wings, whereas the black vulture exhibits a heavy flight with rapid flappings and short glides. Normally its wings are flat. In addition, the turkey vulture has a longer tail than the black and there is extensive white under its wings while the black has white restricted to the wing tips. The turkey vulture is so named because of the bare red skin of the head and neck, which, with the black body, superficially remind one of a turkey. "Buzzard" applies more appropriately to the large hawks of Europe, not to members of the vulture families.

In the eighteenth century both black and turkey vultures were common in both rural areas and most of the large towns in the southern Atlantic states; however, Lawson and Catesby recorded only the turkey vulture.

The usual food is carrion of almost any kind or description for which vultures endlessly search on the wind, soaring overhead in small groups, often circling, while covering enormous areas. The carrion, fresh to putrid, ranges from dead pigs, skunks, and opossums to snakes and fish. These vultures have even been known to kill newly born pigs and baby herons. Although turkey vultures detect much of their prey by sight, it has been demonstrated that this species, unlike the black vulture, can locate food by smell alone. Once a carcass is discovered, great numbers of these birds may descend on it and begin the ghastly feast, tearing off pieces of flesh with their strongly hooked beaks. The black vulture is much more aggressive than the turkey vulture, and blacks may even supplant turkeys at a site of carrion. Catesby noted that "an Eagle sometimes presides at the banquet, and makes them keep their distance while he satiates himself."

Turkey vultures frequently roost in tall trees where they perch silently, wings often outstretched. Catesby noted this behavior and surmised that its purpose was to "purify their filthy carcasses."

The turkey vulture makes little pretense at building a nest, merely depositing two large eggs in a hidden place such as a hollow stump or log, a cave, or even on the ground. The young are fluffy white balls of down.

# EASTERN SCREECH-OWL

*Otus asio*

THE eastern screech-owl, Mark Catesby's "Little Owl," is a resident species across most of central and eastern United States. It is the smallest owl with ear tufts in the region.

Eastern screech-owls are approximately seven to ten inches long and come in two color phases, red and gray. While the sexes are alike in each phase, a given brood may produce both red and gray individuals, and red individuals may mate with gray ones.

These beautiful little owls are at home in a great variety of habitats including orchards, woodlots, suburbs, farms, and wooded streams. Eastern screech-owls prefer conifers but are also found in deciduous woodlands. They are strictly nocturnal and are therefore more often heard than seen. Screech-owls remain hidden most of the day; when nighttime comes, they emerge to hunt for food, flying over meadows and open lands searching for mice, shrews, and insects. Occasionally a bat, snake, or frog is taken.

On moonlit nights they will answer each other from various parts of an orchard or open field, uttering their characteristic melancholy quivering wail that is often described as a descending whistle. From time immemorial the screech-owl's call has been considered an omen of ill luck or even of impending death.

In May the screech-owl begins to construct its nest in the hollow of a tree. The four white eggs soon hatch into small fluffy white balls of down.

Mark Catesby recorded but a single species, the screech-owl, although he surely knew of other owls from their calls in the wilderness. Lawson mentioned the screech-owl and several other types, noting that the "Scritch Owls" were much the same as in Europe; he also stated that "of Owls we have two sorts; the smaller sort is like ours in *England*; the other sort is as big as a middling Goose, and has a prodigious Head. They make a fearful Hollowing in the Night-time, like a Man, whereby they often make Strangers lose their way in the Woods."

The large resident owls of the southern Atlantic states include the great horned owl, barred owl, and barn owl. The great horned owl emits a loud series of deep hoots described as *oot-too-hoo, hoo-hoo,* while the frequently heard barred owl sings a pleasant *who-cooks-for-you, who-cooks-for-you.* The barn owl has a charactcristic raspy, hissing call.

The Passenger Pigeon by Mark Catesby.

# Extinct Species

# PASSENGER PIGEON

*Ectopistes migratorius*

THE last passenger pigeon died in captivity in the Cincinnati Zoological Garden in 1914 after having lived for twenty-nine years. Thus ended the story of one of the most remarkable birds ever to exist on this continent. In 1955 A. W. Schorger estimated that at the time of the discovery of North America, the passenger pigeon population was three to five billion and made up approximately 25 to 40 percent of the entire bird population of the continent.

This beautiful bird, which Catesby called the "Pigeon of Passage" because of its migratory habits, resembled the common mourning dove somewhat but was much larger and more brightly colored, with more blue in the male. Both sexes had a beautiful blue rump.

The passenger pigeon was distributed widely over the eastern part of forested North America, primarily in the north central states. It bred in the northern part of its range and then migrated to the southern Atlantic and Gulf states to spend the winter. The passenger pigeon nested much like the mourning dove, with as many as fifty to one hundred individuals in a single tree. The nest was a simple twig structure in which only a single egg was laid. This species was as well known during the colonial period for the huge migrations that darkened the skies of the southern Atlantic states for days on end as it was for the sheer numbers in the breeding colonies.

Catesby described the migrations: "In *Virginia* I have seen them fly in such continued trains three days successively, that there was not the least interval in losing sight of them." Lawson noted that passenger pigeons appeared in enormous waves during extremely cold winters. He saw such flocks in January and February 1701 near the Cape Fear River. Where the birds roosted, said Lawson, "they had broke down the Limbs of a great many large Trees all over those Woods, . . . wherever these Fowl come in such Numbers, as I saw them then, they clear all before them, scarce leaving one Acorn upon the Ground." In Virginia roosting passenger pigeons "break down the limbs of Oaks with their weight, and leave their dung some inches thick under the trees they roost on," noted Catesby.

Vast numbers of passenger pigeons were killed in the breeding colonies. The squabs were highly prized because the Indians and colonists could melt down their fat to use as a substitute for butter and lard. By the mid-1800s the population of passenger pigeons had begun to undergo a great decline, one from which it never recovered. Man's massive destruction of the birds and of the mature hardwood forests where they nested, combined with the fact that only one egg was produced at a time, resulted in the extinction of this lovely pigeon that once was responsible for one of the most extraordinary natural history scenes on the North American continent.

The Carolina Parakeet by Mark Catesby.

# CAROLINA PARAKEET

*Conuropsis carolinensis*

DURING colonial times the now extinct Carolina parakeet roamed widely over much of the United States, from Florida north along the Atlantic coast up to southern Virginia (rarely to Pennsylvania and New York) and to parts west. Although numerous during the colonial period, the species rapidly declined in numbers and Audubon lamented the scarcity of the parakeet in places where it had been abundant twenty years before. The last parakeets were reported for certain in Florida in 1920, although there were unsubstantiated reports from the Santee Swamp in South Carolina in the 1930s. The Carolina parakeet was successfully bred in captivity, but the last captive bird died in the Cincinnati zoo in 1914.

The only native North American member of the parrot family was a truly resplendent bird with a body of vivid green, a bright yellow head, and an area of scarlet around the base of its bill. Obviously it could not be confused with any other bird and was very well known to colonial travelers. One of the first reports of the parakeet came from Thomas Harriot in 1588: "There are also Parats, Faulcons and Marlin huakes . . ." An interesting later account was from William Hilton, who reported great flocks of parakeets in Carolina: "We kill'd of wild-fowl, four Swans, ten Geese, twenty nine Cranes, ten Turkies, forty Duck and Mallard, three dozen of Parrakeeto's." There is no indication that the Carolina parakeet underwent any appreciable decline in the eighteenth century.

What was the reason for the demise of this beautiful and unique bird? The answer comes from its infamous habits: the Carolina parakeet was a scoundrel. Huge flocks descended on farmers' orchards and cornfields, indiscriminately destroying the fruit and grain. Lawson was familiar with the parakeets' destructive powers: "They peck the Apples, to eat the Kernels, so that the Fruit rots and perishes. They are mischievous to Orchards. They are often taken alive, and will become familiar and tame in two days." Catesby noted: "The orchards in autumn are visited by numerous flights of them, where they make great destruction for their kernels only."

As a consequence, enormous numbers of parakeets were killed, and, to make matters worse, they were also hunted as game because they were considered good to eat. And since they were beautiful, Carolina parakeets were in great demand by professional bird dealers who sold them for cage birds as well as to the millinery trade. The Carolina parakeet had the fatal habit of flying to a fallen comrade, a practice that made it possible to destroy entire flocks at a time. Audubon described how several hundred were shot in this manner in a few hours.

The Carolina parakeet also consumed the seeds of the bald cypress and of cockleburs, plants that Catesby and Audubon, respectively, included in their paintings of parakeets.

PRATT
1987

# Introduced Species

# HOUSE SPARROW

*Passer domesticus*

IT was indeed a gloomy day for the ornithology of the New World when the house sparrow, initially called the English sparrow, was introduced into the United States at Brooklyn in 1850 and 1852. By 1870 it had accomplished an incredible colonization throughout nearly all of North America where there was human habitation. These vermin have undergone such an incredible population increase that they can be encountered virtually everywhere in this country.

The house sparrow is not really a true sparrow but belongs to the Old World family of weavers. Unlike the native New World sparrows, weavers build a large, domed nest, usually with a hole in the side through which the bird enters. House sparrows place their large nests of grasses, string, newspaper, and chicken feathers under almost any type of house eave or similar structure. They lay four to seven eggs. This large clutch size combined with the numerous broods raised per year makes the house sparrow one of the most prolific species in North America. These aggressive birds usurp nesting boxes intended for bluebirds, purple martins, and woodpeckers and consume huge quantities of food that would otherwise be available for other species.

In contrast to the female, which is a dull streaked brown above and dirty white or buffy below, the male house sparrow has a chestnut back and wings, a gray crown, and a black bib.

# EUROPEAN STARLING

*Sturnus vulgaris*

IN 1890 a shipment of sixty starlings arrived in New York City from Europe. These pests, which now cover the entire United States, proliferated from that initial population and an additional forty birds released only a year later.

The European starling belongs to the Old World starling family, a group commonly found in Asia and Africa. The bird is an iridescent black glossed with purple and green and has a yellow bill during the breeding season. In fresh fall plumage its feathers are tipped with some white and buffy color, producing a speckled appearance; as the feather tips wear off, the plumage begins to appear blackish. The juvenile is brown all over, paler below. The species is distinguished in flight by its short tail and stocky appearance.

Starlings lay four or five bluish eggs in natural tree cavities, woodpecker nests, or nesting boxes, causing the native species to abandon their nests and subsequently not raise a brood. Starlings cause tremendous damage to city buildings, roosting and nesting in the cornices and casting their droppings down the sides and onto automobiles below. The introduction of the house sparrow and starling into the New World have become two of the worst "natural" tragedies of our time.

PRATT
1987

# BIBLIOGRAPHY

Allen, E. G. *The History of American Ornithology before Audubon.* American Philosophical Society, *Transactions*, N.S., XLI (1951), pp. 385-391.

American Ornithologists' Union. *Check-list of North American Birds.* 6th ed. Lawrence, Kans.: Allen Press, 1983.

Audubon, John James. *The Birds of America; from original drawings . . .* Vols. I-IV. London: published by the author 1827-1838. (Double elephant folio.)

Bartram, William. *Travels through North and South Carolina, Georgia, East and West Florida, . . .* Philadelphia, 1791.

Bent, Arthur Cleveland. *Life Histories of North American Birds.* U. S. National Museum Bulletins. 21 vols. Washington, D. C.: U. S. Government Printing Office, 1919-1968.

Brickell, John. *The Natural History of North-Carolina . . .* Dublin, 1737.

Burleigh, Thomas Dearborn. *Georgia Birds.* Norman, Okla.: University of Oklahoma Press, 1958.

Byrd, William. *William Byrd's National History of Virginia; or, The Newly Discovered Eden.* Edited and translated by Richmond Croom Beatty and William J. Mulloy from the German *Neu-gefundenes Eden* (1737). Richmond, Va.: Dietz Press, 1940.

————. *Histories of the Dividing Line Betwixt Virginia and North Carolina.* Edited by William K. Boyd. Raleigh, N. C.: North Carolina Historical Commission, 1929.

Catesby, Mark. *The Natural History of Carolina, Florida and the Bahama Islands . . .* 2 vols. London: printed for the author, 1731, 1743.

Dutton, Joan Parry. *Plants of Colonial Williamsburg: How To Identify 200 of Colonial America's Flowers, Herbs, and Trees.* Williamsburg, Va.: Colonial Williamsburg Foundation, 1977.

Elman, Robert. *First in the Field: America's Pioneering Naturalists.* New York: Van Nostrand Reinhold Co., 1977.

*Field Guide to the Birds of North America.* Washington, D. C.: National Geographic Society, 1983.

Frick, George Frederick, and Raymond Phineas Stearns. *Mark Catesby: The Colonial Audubon.* Urbana, Ill.: University of Illinois Press, 1961.

Hariot, Thomas. *A briefe and true report of the new found land of Virginia . . .* London, 1588.

Howell, Arthur Holmes. *Florida Bird Life.* New York: Coward-McCann, 1932.

Jefferson, Thomas. *Notes on the State of Virginia* (1784). Edited by William Peden. Chapel Hill, N. C.: University of North Carolina Press, 1955.

Josselyn, John. *New Englands rarities discovered . . .* London, 1672.

————. *An account of two voyages to New-England . . .* London, 1675.

Lawson, Hugh T., and William S. Powell. *Colonial North Carolina: A History.* New York: Charles Scribner's Sons, 1973.

Lawson, John. *A New voyage to Carolina.* . . . (1709). Edited by Hugh T. Lefler. Chapel Hill, N. C.: University of North Carolina Press, 1967.

Lowery, George Hines. *Louisiana Birds.* Baton Rouge, La.: Louisiana State University Press, 1955.

Morton, Thomas. *New English Canaan* (1632). Reprinted in Peter Force, ed., *Tracts and Other Papers, Relating Principally to the Origin, Settlement, and Progress of the Colonies in North America* . . . Vol. II. Washington, D. C., 1838.

Mosby, Henry Sackett, and Charles O. Handley. *The Wild Turkey in Virginia: Its Status, Life History and Management.* Richmond, Va.: Pittman-Robertson Projects, 1943.

Peterson, Roger Tory. *A Field Guide to the Birds: A Completely New Guide to All the Birds of Eastern and Central North America.* 4th ed. Boston: Houghton Mifflin, 1980.

Potter, Eloise F., James F. Parnell, and Robert P. Teulings. *Birds of the Carolinas.* Chapel Hill, N. C.: University of North Carolina Press, 1980.

Quinn, David B., ed. *The Roanoke Voyages 1584-1590.* London: Cambridge University Press, 1955.

Salley, Alexander Samuel, Jr., ed. *Narratives of Early Carolina, 1650-1708.* New York: Scribner, 1911.

Schorger, A. W. *The Passenger Pigeon.* Madison, Wis.: University of Wisconsin Press, 1955.

Sparks, Jared. *The Works of Benjamin Franklin* . . . Vol. X. Boston, 1840.

Sprunt, Alexander, Jr. *Florida Bird Life.* New York: Coward-McCann, 1954.

Sprunt, Alexander, Jr., and E. Burnham Chamberlain. *South Carolina Bird Life.* Columbia, S. C.: University of South Carolina Press, 1949.

Stearns, Raymond Phineas. *Science in the British Colonies of North America.* Urbana, Ill.: University of Illinois Press, 1970.

Terres, John K. *The Audubon Society Encyclopedia of North American Birds.* New York: Alfred A. Knopf, 1980.

Wilson, Alexander. *American Ornithology; or, the Natural History of the Birds of the United States.* 9 vols. Philadelphia: Bradford and Inskeep, 1808-1814.

# INDEX